Contours of Christian Philosophy
C. STEPHEN EVANS, *Series Editor*

Contours of Christian Philosophy
C. STEPHEN EVANS, *Series Editor*

Philosophy of Religion

Thinking about Faith

C. Stephen Evans

InterVarsity Press
Downers Grove, Illinois, U.S.A.
Leicester, England

InterVarsity Press
P.O. Box 1400, Downers Grove, Illinois 60515, U.S.A.
38 De Montfort Street, Leicester LE1 7GP, England

InterVarsity Press, U.S.A., is the book-publishing division of Inter-Varsity Christian Fellowship, a student movement active on campus at hundreds of universities, colleges and schools of nursing. For information about local and regional activities, write Public Relations Dept., InterVarsity Christian Fellowship, 6400 Schroeder Road, Madison, WI 53707-7895.

Inter-Varsity Press, England, is the publishing division of the Universities and Colleges Christian Fellowship (formerly the Inter-Varsity Fellowship), a student movement linking Christian Unions in universities and colleges throughout the British Isles, and a member movement of the International Fellowship of Evangelical Students. For information about local and national activities in Great Britain write to UCCF, 38 De Montfort Street, Leicester LE1 7GP.

ISBNs: USA 0-87784-343-0   USA 0-87784-339-2 (Contours of Christian Philosophy set)
            UK 0-85110-742-7

Printed in the United States of America

Library of Congress Cataloging in Publication Data

Evans, C. Stephen.
  Philosophy of religion.

  (Contours of Christian philosophy)
  Bibliography: p.
  1. Religion—Philosophy.   2. Philosophical theology.
I. Title.   II. Series.
BL51.E86   1985   200'.1   84-25198
ISBN 0-87784-343-0

British Library Cataloguing in Publication Data

Evans, C. Stephen
  Philosophy of religion: thinking about faith.
  —(Contours of Christian philosophy)
  1. Religion—Philosophy
  I. Title   II. Series
  200'.1   BL51

    ISBN 0-85110-742-7

| 28 | 27 | 26 | 25 | 24 | 23 | 22 | 21 | 20 | 19 | 18 | 17 | 16 | 15 | 14 | 13 |
| 13 | 12 | 11 | 10 | 09 | 08 | 07 | 06 | 05 | 04 | 03 | 02 | 01 | 00 | 99 | |

To Charles

GENERAL PREFACE

The Contours of Christian Philosophy series will consist of short introductory-level textbooks in the various fields of philosophy. These books will introduce readers to major problems and alternative ways of dealing with those problems. These books, however, will differ from most in that they will evaluate alternative viewpoints not only with regard to their general strength, but also with regard to their value in the construction of a Christian world and life view. Thus, the books will explore the implications of the various views for Christian theology as well as the implications that Christian convictions might have for the philosophical issues discussed. It is crucial that Christians attain a greater degree of philosophical awareness in order to improve the quality of general scholarship and evangelical theology. My hope is that this series will contribute to that end.

Although the books are intended as examples of Christian scholarship, it is hoped that they will be of value to others as well; these issues should concern all thoughtful persons. The assumption which underlies this hope is that complete neutrality in philosophy is neither possible nor desirable. Philosophical work always reflects a person's deepest commitments. Such commitments, however, do not preclude a genuine striving for critical honesty.

C. Stephen Evans
Series Editor

1

What Is Philosophy of Religion?

*R*eligion is an important force in human life and human history. This remains the case despite periodic announcements by "secularist" thinkers that humanity has finally come of age and has no more use for religion. Most human beings are still vitally concerned with such questions as "Is there a God?" "Why does God allow suffering?" and "What happens to a person at death?" These and other questions posed by the great religions of the world are grounded in some of the deepest human hopes and fears.

The philosophy of religion can perhaps be best defined in a preliminary way as the attempt to think hard and deeply about such fundamental questions as these. In saying that philosophy of religion focuses on these *questions,* I mean, of course, to say that the *answers* given by religions are also to be the object of attention. Philosophy of religion is therefore critical reflection on religious *beliefs.*

To explain why the focus of philosophy of religion is on religious beliefs, it would be helpful to say a little more about both philosophy and religion. Philosophy and religion are sometimes viewed as rivals, and the relations between them have not always been cordial. Some of the reasons for this mutual suspicion will become clear as we proceed. The questions "What is philosophy?" and "What is religion?" are, of course, enormously difficult. Such complex human activities can obviously be defined in many different ways. Indeed, it is possible to define "philosophy" and "religion" in such a way that they become mutually exclusive rivals. Religious believers have sometimes seen philosophers as unsympathetic critics who try to undermine religious faith. To the believer the philosopher may appear as a presumptuous champion of human reason who rejects divine wisdom. Conversely, the philosopher has sometimes seen the religious believer as a benighted defender of superstition and blind obedience to authority.

While these kinds of conflicts have certainly occurred, and though tensions between philosophy and religion remain, it would be a great mistake to embody such oppositions in the very definitions of "philosophy" and "religion." Conflict is not inevitable. Some of the greatest philosophers have been religious believers, and some of the greatest contributions to religious thought have come from philosophers—religious and nonreligious. The question of whether religion is reasonable, or whether it should even try to be, is among the questions which philosophy of religion aims to answer. Such inquiries should not be settled in a peremptory fashion by the way we define our terms.

Religion is a complicated and rich human phenomenon, and as such it is studied by academicians from many disciplines: historians, psychologists, sociologists and theologians, to name a few. Religion touches on the whole of human existence. A practicing adherent of a particular religion has not only certain characteristic beliefs but also characteristic emotions, attitudes and experiences. The believer usually associates with other believers in a community that may be relatively loose or extraordinarily tight-knit. The believer usually acts differently from the nonbeliever. He engages in worship and other religious exercises. He may attempt to follow a set of rules or principles throughout life; he may take as a role model the life of the founder of the religion.

Religion can by no means then be reduced to a purely intellectual phenomenon. A religion is not simply a set of beliefs or dogmas. However, most religions at least include beliefs. A religious person does not merely have different feelings or attitudes. She thinks differently about herself and her world.* She worships as part of a community, and that community is defined in part by its beliefs.

We will say more later about philosophy, but philosophy has always been understood as a search for wisdom or knowledge. The philosopher is a seeker of truth, and it is therefore natural for this "belief" element of religion to catch the eye of the philosopher. The philosopher wants to know whether religious beliefs are true and whether they can be known to be true or reasonably believed to be true. In considering these religious beliefs, of course, the philosopher ought not to wrench them out of context, but to see them in relation to other elements of religious life. (Philosophers have not always followed this rule.) The philosopher's main interest, however, will be such religious beliefs as "God created the world" and "Human beings are destined for eternal life."

Philosophy of Religion and Other Disciplines
This focus on the truth and reasonableness of religious belief

---

*In this book I have chosen to employ both masculine and feminine pronouns. I hope readers who find this jarring will understand and excuse the convention, which is adopted out of consideration for readers who find the exclusive use of the masculine pronouns disturbing.

helps distinguish the philosophy of religion from other academic disciplines that study religion. While the historian or sociologist may also study religious beliefs, his focus is not specifically on the truth or reasonableness of such beliefs. False beliefs may be as important as true ones to the historian or sociologist who tries to paint a picture of the history of a religion or the place of religion in society.

The distinction between the philosopher of religion and the theologian is trickier. Theology is an activity carried on *within* religion (at least in theory). Thus the theologian looks at religious beliefs from within, as an adherent or representative of a religious tradition. Philosophy of religion, on the other hand, as critical reflection on religious questions and beliefs, may be engaged in by thinkers who are not themselves religious at all, as well as by committed religious thinkers. (We will shortly deal with the question as to whether this critical reflection can and should be done from a neutral perspective.)

This initial distinction between theology and the philosophy of religion is not quite acceptable as it stands, primarily because there is more than one kind of theology. What was said above applies at least roughly to the theologian of an actual religion. For example, Christian theology includes the overlapping categories of dogmatic theology, biblical theology and systematic theology. A theologian who engages in any of these may in fact do some philosophy of religion, but that is not his main business. There is also, however, the kind of theology called *natural theology* (sometimes called *philosophical theology*), in which the theologian attempts to say what can be known about God or things divine apart from any commitment to any particular religion, claims to special revelation and so on. Natural theology in this sense cannot be sharply separated from the philosophy of religion, inasmuch as a good part of the philosophy of religion consists in defenses of or attacks on natural theology. Still the two disciplines are not identical, as can be seen from the fact that one of the issues in philosophy of religion is whether natural theology is truly vital to religion, as well as whether it can be successfully carried out. Philosophy of religion as a task will still be necessary even if natural theology is abandoned.

Philosophy of Religion and Philosophy

In addition to distinguishing the philosophy of religion from theology and from the empirical disciplines that study religion as "factual" (history, psychology and sociology), it is important to distinguish the philosophy of religion from religious philosophies. To draw this distinction, a little more must be said about philosophy in general.

It is often pointed out by philosophers that the question "What is philosophy?" is itself part of philosophy. Philosophers do not agree among themselves about what philosophy is. Hence it is probably impossible to give a completely neutral definition of philosophy, a definition which does not itself presuppose some philosophical commitments.

Some philosophers attempt to get around the obvious substantive disagreements among philosophers by specifying some supposedly neutral method of answering the questions of philosophy. This method can then be assumed as the common ground in terms of which philosophy can be defined. Unfortunately, however, there is almost as much disagreement about the proper method for philosophy as about the conclusions of philosophy. Rationalists propose that philosophy should employ a method of deductive proof, linguistic philosophers think philosophy should consist of the analysis of language, and phenomenologists think that philosophy should concern itself with the description of "lived" experience. None of these methods really appears to be purely neutral either, because when unpacked they invariably presuppose a particular view of reason or language or experience.

Perhaps a beginning can be made by noting what we have

already claimed and what all the different schools of philosophy
seem to admit: philosophy is a rational enterprise. Whatever else
it may be, philosophy is a reflective activity; philosophy is a kind
of thinking. Of course, not every kind of thinking will qualify
as philosophical. No one would dignify my thinking about what
kind of toothpaste to use with the label "philosophy." The thinking we call philosophy is an unusually serious kind of thinking,
directed to especially serious kinds of problems.

Certain kinds of questions seem to be asked by almost all
human beings who have reached a certain level of reflectiveness.
Who am I? What kind of a world do I live in? What is worth
living for? These foundational questions have a universal
significance, and they properly inspire the deepest and most
rigorous kind of thinking. Answers to them, especially when
those answers are comprehensive and organized, are called
philosophies. And the activity of seriously wrestling with these
questions is called philosophy.

Some of the organized systematic answers to basic human
questions have an undeniably religious flavor to them. In some
cases the answers are taken directly from a religious tradition.
Other philosophies seem to have been developed in response to
religion; they seek to answer the same questions and meet the
same needs and therefore may be seen as rivals to religion. Both
types of philosophies may properly be called religious. Religious
philosophy then is philosophical thinking which is religious in
inspiration or direction.

Religious philosophy in this sense is not identical with the
philosophy of religion. As a form of reflection, philosophy is
always self-conscious and critical. The philosopher not only
builds systems of thought; he critically reflects on those systems.
It is this critical and reflective side of philosophy that is most
evident in the philosophy of religion. Philosophy of religion is
not so much religious thinking as it is thinking *about* religion,
a thinking which can be carried on by both religious and

nonreligious persons.

Can Thinking about Religion Be Neutral?

We have differentiated philosophy of religion from theology and religious philosophy by describing it as a reflective activity that requires a certain critical distance from its subject. In comparison with theology and religious philosophy, the philosophy of religion appears to aim for a neutral stance. But is such neutrality with respect to religious matters really possible? Some religious thinkers have denied that it is, claiming, for example, that a human being cannot be neutral with respect to God. The person who is not properly submissive to God is, they claim, a rebel. "He who is not for us is against us."

Even more radically, one might ask whether such neutrality is desirable. Is it not possible that those who attempt to adopt a neutral, disinterested posture cut themselves off from the possibility of even understanding what religion is all about?

Posing these questions puts us right into the heart of a central question in the philosophy of religion *and* theology, the problem of the relation of faith to reason. One's view of faith and reason largely determines whether one sees philosophy and religion as inevitably hostile to each other, as coexisting peacefully but independently, or as possible allies. Chapter eight attempts to deal with this issue more fully, but it is necessary for two reasons to say something about it at the very outset of a book such as this.

First, some religious believers hold a view of faith and reason which claims that rational reflection on religion is impossible, useless or even harmful. In effect, they call into question the very legitimacy of philosophy of religion. Hence some consideration of their view is in order if we are to be truly reflective and critical. Second, it seems only fair to try to become clear, and to help the reader become clear, about the standpoint taken by this book. What kind of thinking about religion is going on in these pages?

I shall approach this issue first (returning to it in chapter eight) by sketching two opposing viewpoints, *fideism* and *neutralism*. These I will criticize and reject. I will then propose an alternative which will, I hope, preserve the strengths and eliminate the weaknesses of the initial theories. This constructive proposal will be termed *critical dialog*.

Fideism

Many theologians have claimed that human beings are inherently religious. If they do not worship the true God, then they worship false gods—themselves, or things of their own making. On this view a human being is never religiously neutral; he is always either a faithful servant or a rebel against the Creator. The faithful servant functions as he was meant to function and fulfills his created destiny. The rebel, however, is always "kicking against the pricks." All her activities reflect the distorted and twisted character she has given to life.

Some have concluded from this that the thinking of the unbeliever is also twisted and distorted, either in all areas or at least with respect to essential moral and religious truth. Although the reasoning of rebellious humans makes a pretense of neutrality, this neutrality is in fact an illusion. Indeed, the very attempt of humans to think about God "for themselves," independently and autonomously, is proof of their rebelliousness. It represents an attempt on the part of man to put his own thought and reason above God.

This view implies that human attempts to reflect on the truth of religious beliefs are disastrous. It is impossible for the unbeliever as an unbeliever to reflect on the reasonableness of religious belief and thereby become a believer. Rather, the unbeliever's only hope is first to *believe* and then perhaps come to see the reasonableness of the belief. If God in his mercy reveals to the unbeliever the truth about himself and the unbeliever, the unbeliever must humbly accept this truth. God must "force an entry." The unbeliever's twisted thinking can only be straightened out as his status and life change from that of rebel to servant. Only the regenerate mind can see the truth.

This view implies that one cannot arrive at true religious beliefs as a result of rational reflection. The starting place for any correct thinking about religion is rather a genuine faith, a personal commitment. Fideism claims that faith is the precondition for any correct thinking about religion.[1]

Fideism puts its critics in an awkward spot, for all criticism of the view can easily be written off as the product of unbelief. It thus gains an invulnerable status against all attacks. But it gains this status at a rather high cost; the fideist cannot attempt to win over his critics by rational argument or even attempt to engage in rational dialog with those who disagree. The presupposition of such dialog and argument is the possibility of common ground, some point of agreement which can be reflected on or appealed to. But it is just this kind of common ground which the fideist denies.

The attitude of the fideist resembles in an interesting way the attitude of some orthodox Marxists, who dismiss the criticisms of Marxism made by non-Marxist economists, political scientists and philosophers. The Marxist reasons that these people are committed to the economic status quo and that their criticisms are therefore merely an ideological smokescreen which hides economic self-interest. If a Marxist holds to this position universally in a rigid a priori manner, he eliminates any true dialog between Marxists and non-Marxists. The orthodox Marxist loses the benefit of criticism which might enable him to improve his theories. He shuts himself up in a sterile "world of the committed" and thereby loses the chance to show non-Marxists that Marxism really does provide a superior framework for interpreting political and economic events. In the long run his party-line theories do not develop, and eventually they are accepted only by those who find it expedient to do so, and by those who know no alternatives.

In an analogous way the fideist also encloses herself within "the world of the committed," and in a similar manner she eliminates the possibility of showing the nonbeliever the superiority of a religious world view. But fideism faces an even more serious problem: Where should one place one's faith? To what should one be committed?

In effect, the fideist says, "Commit yourself and you will see that what I say is true." The problem is that *many* people say that, asking for commitment to many different things. One can demand commitment to creeds, books, churches or popes. Religious sects, political ideologies (like Marxism), psychological cults and non-Christian religions all make their appeals.

The Christian fideist may, of course, respond that there is an important difference between his commitments and those of all other faiths. He holds to the *true* set of beliefs, the *right* presuppositions. He can see the truth because he has been regenerated; he has the witness of the Spirit. Of course, these claims may be correct, but how does one know them to be correct? Adherents of other religions can easily make similar claims.

It seems to me that in a pluralistic culture it is almost impossible *not* to reflect critically on where one should place one's trust. And even if it is possible to make a commitment apart from critical reflection, the existence of even one Jonestown horror would make it clear that it is irresponsible not to exercise critical judgment when asked for commitment. To the sincere individual who really wants truth, the fideist offers no help; he offers only another voice crying out in the middle of the modern religious babel.

Perhaps the mistake of the fideist is to overestimate dogmatically the impact of unbelief. For the moment let us concede that most (or all) human beings are rebels against God. Let us further concede that this status impairs their personality in all its functions, including their reasoning. From this it follows only that it may be difficult for human beings in this condition to think rightly about God. Their thinking may be harmed and limited in all kinds of ways, but it does not necessarily follow that such thinking is useless. After all, God remains God, the Creator, and he may well establish limits to the ways in which even a rebellious creature may run amuck in his thinking.

At the very least it seems wrong-headed to conclude at the outset that human thinking about God is worthless. Perhaps this is a conclusion one might be wearily driven to accept, after many efforts, but even then it would appear that human thinking would have to have a certain competence *even to recognize its incompetence.* Such a negative result might, in fact, be a valuable conclusion, analogous to the wisdom of Socrates, who surpassed his contemporaries by recognizing what he did not know.

But what about the charge of the fideist that critical thinking about religious belief is impious or presumptuous, an arrogant placing of human reason above God? It would seem that whether critical reflection about religious questions is presumptuous depends chiefly on two factors. The first is whether God, if real, wants humans to reflect about religious truth. If God had forbidden humans to think critically about religious questions, then perhaps it would be impious to do so, provided one had some way of knowing about the prohibition. But I see absolutely no reason to think that God wishes human beings to suppress their critical faculties. After all, our ability to think is a gift from God, and it seems proper to assume that this gift, like others God has bestowed, is intended to be used if used properly. And it would certainly appear to be a proper use of reason, when confronted by a plurality of competing truth-claims, to reflect on matters as important as religious belief.

The second factor which would affect whether critical thinking about religion is legitimate is the manner in which the thinking is carried on. Clearly it is possible to think about God (or anything else) in an arrogant or presumptuous manner. No doubt much actual human thinking about God is of this character. But this is surely a temptation to combat, not a necessary feature of critical thought about religion. A person who sincerely wants to know whether God is real, who is willing to recognize his own inferior status in relation to God, who recognizes the fallibility and possible bias of his own thinking, who understands that it is unlikely that he will be able to gain a fully adequate understanding of God, who is open to the possibility that his thinking may have to be aided by God to be successful, and who thereby does not rule out the possibility of a revelation—such a person's thinking about God would hardly appear to be impious or presumptuous.

Neutralism

The opposite pole from the fideist is the philosopher who insists that our thinking about religious matters must be presuppositionless. The neutralist believes that our critical thinking will only be likely to help us toward the truth if it is completely impartial and unbiased. Thus to think rightly about religious matters we must put aside all our commitments, or at least those commitments which are religiously "loaded," and adopt a completely neutral stance.

The neutralist in effect claims that to be reasonable is to think without making any "risky" assumptions. Two sorts of questions must be asked about this. First, if the neutralist is right, is it possible to think reasonably? *Can* human beings think in a purely neutral, disinterested manner? Second, is the neutralist right? Does reason require that one jettison all prior commitments and assumptions?

With regard to the first type of question, it is painfully obvious that human thinking is very much affected by all sorts of nonrational factors. Our thought is colored not only by our prior experiences but by our emotions, our upbringing and education, the ideas and attitudes of our friends, our historical situation, and a host of other factors. It is true that by reflection we can become conscious of some of these factors and negate or reduce their influence. But it seems unlikely that a person could ever do this completely. Indeed, it would seem foolish and unreasonable for a person to believe she has done this, for such a self-satisfied attitude would harm her chances of uncovering other nonrational influences. I conclude that the proposal of the neutralist cannot be accepted as a condition or requirement of rational thought. It can be at most an ideal which one should strive to approximate.

But, second, is neutralism even valid as an ideal? Is the neutralist right to insist that rational thought be presupposition-less? A full treatment of this question would require a detailed discussion of the central issues in the theory of knowledge.[2] Such an excursion into epistemology is hardly possible here, but it is necessary to say something about these questions, even if what is said is very sketchy.

A long and venerable philosophical tradition holds that genuine knowledge must consist of truths which are known with absolute certainty. We shall term this view *foundationalism*, using the term in a "strong" sense.[3] To know something, one must have a conclusive reason to think it is true. But of course one must also know that the reason is a good one, and therefore one must know it to be true, which may require a reason for one's reason. This threatens to become an infinite regress unless one knows some things directly or immediately, things which there-fore can be said to be basic or foundational to knowledge. If this foundational knowledge is not really known but is merely be-lieved or assumed, then the whole structure of knowledge be-comes insecure. For this reason, the foundationalist insists that this basic knowledge must be certain. Any proposal to begin with unjustified or unproven assumptions, as the fideist recom-mends, is disastrous. Only what can be recognized to be true with certainty by a purely objective thinker will do.

We have already discussed whether such thinking is really possible. We are now asking whether it is desirable. Perhaps one way of getting a handle on this question is to see how well the foundationalist ideal accurately describes the work of natural scientists. Most people would agree that in the natural sciences people are working toward knowledge in a rational manner. However, many philosophers of science would today question whether scientists follow the foundationalist ideal.

It has always been evident that scientists make some assumptions which do not seem unquestionable and which cannot really be proven to be true. They assume that nature is basically intelligible and orderly. A uniformity of natural processes and of experience is also assumed as a basis for making generalizations. However, in addition to these very general assumptions, it seems quite plausible to claim that science only progresses if more specific kinds of commitments are made. T. S. Kuhn, in his book *The Structure of Scientific Revolutions,* has called attention to the way "normal science" depends on what he terms a *paradigm,* a basic set of assumptions which is embodied in the practices of a scientific community.[4] Kuhn argues convincingly that the acceptance of such a paradigm is not simply a matter of "checking it by the facts," as the foundationalist might wish to claim, since the basic paradigm beliefs have at least some bearing on what is to count as a fact and how the facts are to be described. As some interpret him, Kuhn goes on to make the extreme and questionable claim that the adoption of a paradigm is a nonrational matter governed by sociological factors. Even if one does not accept this extreme claim, Kuhn's work still implies that science, far from precluding less-than-certain commitments, actually depends on such commitments.

The history of philosophy also provides an interesting way of testing the claims of the foundationalist. Perhaps the philosopher who most rigorously attempted to follow the foundationalist program was René Descartes (1596-1650). Descartes attempted to realize the ideal of pure objectivity by methodically subjecting all his beliefs to doubt. By supposing that all his experiences might be dream experiences and that it was possible that he was constantly being deceived by an evil being of great power, Descartes rejected almost all his previous beliefs as uncertain. All that remained was the certain truth of his own existence, which he affirmed to be undoubtable as long as he was conscious.

With this slender foundation of "I think, therefore I am," Descartes attempted to prove the existence of God, the external world and his own immaterial soul. However, almost no one today finds Descartes' arguments convincing. It seems evident, rather, that David Hume was correct in asserting that Cartesian doubt would be incurable if attainable.[5] Rather than laying a foundation for knowledge, Descartes' doubt seems a sure road to total skepticism.

Critical Dialog

What option remains? We have rejected both fideism and neutralism, the former because it precludes rational reflection, the latter because it places impossible demands on rational reflection. But there is something correct about both these viewpoints. It can be seen from our criticism of neutralism that the fideist has a valid point when he stresses the way our thought is conditioned by basic assumptions and attitudes. And surely the neutralist has a point against the fideist in stressing the value of honest, no-holds-barred, critical reflection on our commitments. How then can reason and commitment be combined?

Perhaps the two can be brought into a happy if sometimes tension-filled alliance by rethinking what it means to be reasonable. Instead of seeing reason as presuppositionless thinking, suppose we view reason as a *willingness to test one's commitments*. Perhaps the fideist is right in claiming that it is impossible to begin without commitments; perhaps it is not even desirable. But it is a mistake to claim that commitments, even fundamental ones, are impervious to criticism and modification. Perhaps the neutralist is right in urging us to strive to rationally evaluate our commitments, to reflect on them critically and honestly in the light of evidence and argument. But it is a mistake to think that this process of testing can or should proceed from a totally neutral standpoint, the standpoint of a person without any convictions. Although any belief can in principle be doubted, we cannot doubt all our beliefs at once without undermining the possibility of overcoming the doubt.

How does one go about testing one's beliefs? Simple beliefs about particular matters of fact are subject to fairly direct experiential tests. More general and comprehensive scientific theories can only be tested indirectly. One looks for theoretical coherence, predictive power, the ability to illuminate what was previously unintelligible. Usually a theory must be tested relative to its rivals. A scientific theory which explains a great deal will be accepted even if it faces serious objections as long as there is no viable alternative. Sometimes the decision to continue to accept a theory requires one to discount or reinterpret what purport to be facts; at other times it seems more reasonable to accept the fact and reject or modify the theory. In short, the testing of theories is a complicated affair, requiring an element of good judgment as well as honesty and concern for truth. One assumes that experience is not infinitely plastic; some theories fit the facts better than others. But the process of testing is not one for which formal rules can be given.

The testing of basic religious beliefs seems to me to be basically a similar matter, although the kinds of experiences which are relevant as evidence is far broader. The testing of religious beliefs is, of course, likely to be even more difficult than the testing of scientific theories. The reasons for this are many, but they include the point with which the fideist begins.

Few if any people are indifferent to religious matters. Since religion bears on a person's life in a far more direct and personal way than science, one can expect it to be correspondingly more difficult to reach agreement on religious matters. Common ground may be hard to find, and rational discussion may sooner or later reach an impasse where both sides say, "This is how it appears to me."

But though common ground may be difficult to find (or even impossible, as the fideist claims), that is no reason not to *look*. Each person is an individual and no doubt must make a final judgment about "the way things appear to him." But to the extent that one individual has made an effort to engage others in critical dialog, he is entitled to regard his commitments as no longer mere prejudices but as convictions which have withstood a process of critical testing and are so far reasonable. In the process of critical dialog the individual attempts to think through the alternatives and the objections to his own view which those alternatives put forward. In the course of such a process a person's views may be modified or abandoned. What survives is not merely prejudice or bias but, subject to a continued willingness to test what appears doubtful, reasoned conviction.

Such a process cannot be guaranteed to work successfully, of course. Finite, fallible human beings cannot survey all the alternatives or assess those they do examine with total accuracy. And the process of reflection cannot be extended indefinitely. The purpose of our religious beliefs is ultimately to guide our lives; if a person spent all his time critically reflecting on his beliefs, there would be no point in having any in the first place.

Philosophy of religion, I believe, is best viewed as a process of critical dialog. Obviously each participant in the dialog approaches it from her own unique perspective. This means that even her critical reflections about her faith are shaped somewhat by her attitudes, basic convictions and previous experiences. In short, people participate as whole persons, not calculating machines. But the honest participant does not shrink from self-consciously examining any part of what he brings to the encounter. No commitments can be taken off the table as not subject to discussion. And although it may not be possible to be neutral, it is possible for the participants in the dialog to be honest with themselves and others. This honesty requires a willingness to see if the evidence really is best interpreted and explained according to one's own theory.

Such a critical dialog is risky. Probably everyone has heard a story of a student in a strict religious environment who loses his faith as a result of the critical challenges hurled at him at a university. But there is something unhealthy and even dishonest about a faith which hides from such a challenge. Can one really believe in God wholeheartedly and at the same time assert that one can only continue to believe by refusing to consider the evidence against one's belief? Such a "belief" seems perilously close to a half-conscious conviction that in fact God may not be real, combined with a wish to hide this truth from oneself. (Although a decision to ignore evidence must not be confused with an honest recognition of one's inability to properly evaluate evidence. It might be entirely proper for an uneducated person to refuse to consider complicated, abstract arguments which would only confuse and bewilder him.)

A genuine and robust faith will not shrink from the process of testing, for it is confident that it will indeed pass the test. If I genuinely believe that God is real (or that he is an illusion), I will not be afraid to examine alternative views and listen to problems and objections raised by others. Through this process I am confident that my faith will be deepened and strengthened. Furthermore, by listening to my opponent and by looking for common ground on which to show her the superiority of my belief, I gain the possibility of making my opponent into a friend and ally. Instead of churlishly telling those who have other views that they must begin by accepting my presuppositions—an action which is probably not possible even if it were desirable, since belief is not usually under voluntary control—I attempt to find ground on which we both are comfortable. The process may be difficult, and with some it is doubtless impossible. I must not allow my opponent to lure me over the cliff into the thin air of neutralism, where no living human being can stand. But the search for common ground is worth making.

In the following chapters we shall look at the dialog as it has gone on in Western philosophy over a number of issues, including the following: (1) arguments for and against the kind of God believed in by Christians, Jews and Muslims; (2) how religious experience is best analyzed and what we can conclude from it; (3) whether a person could ever be justified in accepting some person, book or creed as having special authority; (4) whether miracles are possible and under what conditions one might believe in their occurrence; (5) how religious language, especially talk about God, can be best understood; (6) finally, we will return to the issue discussed in this chapter, that of personal commitment and intellectual honesty in a religiously pluralistic world.

Obviously this part of the dialog is not comprehensive, and it is not one which would suit every potential participant. The issues addressed are largely those which emerge from a serious consideration of the Christian faith, though many of them have counterparts for those who adhere to other religious traditions. Most of the examples will be taken from Christianity. Thus this book will probably be of more interest to Christians and people seriously interested in Christianity than to those of other faiths. But as an introduction to critical dialog about faith, it is better to focus on the faith one understands best. For most people in the West, that is Christianity. I hope, however, that as an introduction to critical dialog the book will be of value to those of any faith, as well as to those who lack faith in any traditionally religious sense of the term.

The Theistic God:
The Project of
Natural Theology

A belief in God or gods of some kind is central to the great majority of the world's religions. Obviously, then, two key questions for the philosophy of religion are whether it is reasonable to believe in a God and, if so, what kind of a God should be believed in.

Concepts of God

Though there are a great number of views about God which vary tremendously in the details, most views about God can be seen as falling into one of a relatively small number of types. *Polytheism,* the belief that there exists a plurality of personal gods, is common among primitive peoples and is clearly present in Greek and Nordic mythology. *Henotheism* also recognizes a plurality of gods, but the henotheist restricts his allegiance to one god, either because he sees that god in some way as superior to the others or simply because that god is the god of his own tribe or people. *Monotheism,* often simply abbreviated as *theism,* holds that only one God exists. God is seen as a personal being, supreme in power, knowledge and moral worth, who created all other existing beings out of nothing. *Pantheism,* often associated with Hinduism and other Eastern religions but not uncommon in the West, holds that it is not ultimately proper to think of God as a personal being or as a being of any kind. Such concepts are too limiting for God, who must ultimately be understood as identical with nature or the universe as a whole. *Panentheism* says that God is not identical with the universe but must be seen as including the universe. The universe is in some sense God, but God is more than the universe.

These are the major views about God which are found in the religions of the world. There are, of course, many interesting variations on each view, some of which are significant enough to warrant a name. Thus *dualism* can be seen as a variation on polytheism, the dualist holding to a plurality of only two gods who are opposed to each other. (Usually one god is seen as good and the other as evil.) *Deism,* in one of its senses, can be understood as a variation on theism. The deist believes in one God, like the theist, but believes that this God cannot or does not involve himself in his creation. *Absolute monism* can be seen as a variation on pantheism or panentheism. The absolute monist holds that God is an absolute unity which is somehow manifested in a less-than-fully-real world of apparent plurality.

The list of views about God also includes views which reject any kind of a God. *Agnosticism* holds that the truth about God cannot be or is not known and that people should therefore suspend judgment on the question. *Atheism* goes further and actually denies the existence of God. *Naturalism* is simply atheism expressed positively. The atheist does not believe in a God behind nature; he simply believes that the natural order of things exists "on its own." While atheism is a belief held by many antireligious people, it is also sometimes held by religious people. The Theravada variety of Buddhism appears to embrace atheism, and some atheists have attempted to put forward a humanistic "religion of man" which would not involve belief in a God of any kind.

The Theistic Concept of God

Of all the various views of God, monotheism (henceforth theism for short) holds a special importance. It is the dominant view of God in three of the world's great religions: Christianity, Judaism and Islam. Views of God which seem to approximate theism are also found among a significant number of Hindus and Buddhists, and traces or suggestions of such a view can be found in the writings of some of the great philosophers of ancient Greece and in many other religions as well. The reasonableness of theism seems therefore to be an issue well worth considering. Before attempting this, however, we need to say a little more about what a theistic conception of God involves.

In the Judeo-Christian tradition there has emerged a reasonably well-defined list of characteristics which are seen as essential to God. Some of the elements on the list are more central than others, and a person rejecting one or more of them might still be recognized as holding to theism or a variation on it. But there is a good deal of agreement about what God, if he exists, is supposed to be like. God, whatever else he may be, is supposed to be worthy of worship, the supreme object of religious devotion. This requirement seems to have played a key role in the refinement of the theistic concept of God.

It would appear to be a minimal requirement for a being worthy of worship that he be greater than any other being. No other being exceeds God in power, knowledge or goodness. But this requirement is indeed minimal, since theists usually hold that God is not only greater than any other being as a matter of fact, but that it is impossible that there should ever be a being greater than God. God's power, knowledge and goodness are therefore seen not merely as very great but as maximal. God is *omnipotent;* he possesses all the power a being can have. God is *omniscient;* he knows everything which it is possible for a being to know. God is *morally perfect;* his goodness is unsurpassable.

Another way of expressing God's greatness is to say that he is *infinite,* or unlimited. These terms must, however, be understood in a qualified sense. To say that God is infinite in power does not mean that he can literally do anything. It has usually been held, for example, that God cannot create a square circle or a person with a morally free will who is determined always to choose what is morally right. The reason for this is not that God lacks some power or ability he might have had, but that these conceptions are logically contradictory and therefore impossible or even meaningless. God's power is the power to do anything which is logically possible. In addition, most theists hold that there are certain things God cannot do because of his nature. Being morally perfect, he cannot commit an act of senseless cruelty, for example. God's omnipotence must then be understood as the power to do whatever is logically possible and consistent with God's own essential characteristics. Similar restrictions may have to be placed on the concept of omniscience.

Even with these qualifications God's power is still infinite in the sense of being unlimited by anything outside himself. God is in no way limited by any other being. It is for this reason that God is often described as a *necessary* being. God does not just happen to exist. Since nothing can threaten his existence, his nonexistence is not really possible. Theists have understood this necessity in two ways. Some have held that God's existence is logically necessary. On this view "God does not exist" is actually self-contradictory, though it is admitted that the contradiction is not an obvious one. Others have held that God's necessity is simply grounded in his power and independence. Nothing can in fact threaten God's existence, so his existence is factually necessary even if his nonexistence is logically possible. Another way of putting this is to say that God is *self-existent,* meaning literally that his existence depends on nothing outside himself. Sometimes the medieval term *aseity* is used to denote this characteristic of self-existence.

Since God is a necessary being, he is not just "another being." He *is* in some sense a being, however, on the traditional theistic account; not only that, but he is a being of a certain type with a particular nature. God is not just "being-itself"; such descriptions fail to do justice to the *personal* character of God. That God is personal is implicit in what has already been said, because only a personal being can have power, knowledge and moral perfection. To have power is to be able to do things, to act in certain ways. To know things a being must be intelligent, have a mind. To be morally perfect is to be perfect in deeds, intentions and thoughts. Although God certainly surpasses human persons in many respects, and some theists would insist that God is more than personal, it is clear that God cannot be *less* than personal. It is not clear what it would be like for a being to be more than personal. At the least God must be seen as more like a person than anything else humans have experienced.

Since God is personal, it is appropriate to understand him as *acting.* God's primary action is usually understood as that of creation. That God is the *Creator* means not only or even primarily that whatever had a beginning was begun by God, but that whatever exists at any moment exists because of God's will and creative power. Everything which exists other than God depends on God for its existence, a relationship which is properly stated by describing God as Creator and all other things as creatures.

As Creator, God is therefore continuously active in his creation. (The denial of this is a reversion to deism.) This is not to deny a certain autonomy and integrity to the created order, but it does imply that whatever occurs does so because God wills it or permits it to occur. God is everywhere present within his creation in the sense that he can and does bring about events immediately, and he knows what occurs everywhere in the same immediate manner. Therefore it is a mistake to think of God as limited to one region of space. He is properly thought of as *omnipresent*, present everywhere by virtue of his activity and knowledge. Theists have traditionally agreed that this implies that God has no body; he is a *spirit*.

Just as God is not limited by space, so he is in some way not limited by time. God is an *eternal* spirit. There are some important differences in the way theists have understood God's being eternal. Many have thought of eternity as timelessness; God is thought of as having no "before and after." God is outside time altogether. Others have understood God's eternality as "being everlasting." God exists at all times on this view, having neither beginning nor end. He is not limited by time in the sense that it takes him no time to carry out his actions and in the sense that his plans and purposes cannot be dimmed or frustrated by the passage of time. This divergence of views about the nature of God's eternality is not a recent development but goes back hundreds of years. In the twentieth century it has, however, received a sharper form as a result of the development of "process theologies," which emphasize the "before and after" aspect of God's consciousness.

The divergence of views about God's eternality is also reflected in differing views of whether God in any sense changes. Obviously a perfect being must possess a degree of stability; one would not want to worship a God who radically altered his character on a whim. Classically, many theists, especially those who think of God as timelessly eternal, have believed that God is absolutely unchangeable, or *immutable*. On this view change of any kind is incompatible with perfection. Others have understood God's immutability as referring to his essential nature or attributes. God's character and purposes do not change, but he is aware of what goes on in his creation and capable of modifying his responses and actions in light of that awareness.

This then is a brief recounting of the theistic concept of God. God is an eternal, self-existent spirit, unchangeable at least in his basic character and purposes, who exists necessarily. He is a personal being who is omnipotent, omniscient and morally perfect. God is the Creator of all things other than himself, and he is omnipresent in his creation, though without a body.

In recent years philosophers have done a good deal of interesting work on these concepts. Concepts of God have been developed and refined, and their mutual consistency has been debated. The limits of this book do not allow us to go into this debate, even though it is a discussion worth pursuing in a fuller context.[1] My own conclusion is that it would appear reasonable to claim that theism is logically coherent. Although many of the concepts used to characterize God must be carefully defined and qualified, no one has convincingly shown that theism as an overall view is inconsistent. A system of belief which has been accepted by millions of people for centuries is not necessarily true, but it would seem reasonable to claim that the burden of proof rests on anyone who asserts that such a system is self-contradictory. No one has been able to show that theism is self-contradictory. It would seem appropriate, then, to proceed to examine the reasonableness of theism. If we have good reason to believe theism is true, we also have good reason to think it is logically consistent. What grounds do we have for believing that the God of theism exists?

Natural Theology

As we have already pointed out, theism is held in common by Christianity, Judaism and Islam. The relation between theism and a particular religion like Christianity is as follows: If Christianity is true, then theism is true. If theism is true, then

Christianity is not necessarily true, but it may be true, and one might even claim that the probability of Christianity's being true is increased. At the very least, one reason for thinking Christianity to be false is eliminated if theism is true.

Philosophers interested in the reasonableness of a religion like Christianity have therefore often proceeded by first attempting to determine the truth of theism. The idea seems to be that one should first establish the truth of theism and then proceed to determine which, if any, of the theistic religions is true. First one must determine whether God exists, and then one can go on to ask whether God has revealed himself through special events and people. This attempt to determine the truth of theism without assuming the standpoint of a particular religion we shall term *natural theology,* or philosophical theology. The natural theologian attempts to see what can be known about God independently of any special religious authority. The potential value of natural theology for religious apologetics is evident, since it will be far easier to argue that some individual or book is a revelation from God if it is antecedently known (or probable) that there is a God.

Although natural theology seems worth pursuing, it is by no means evident that this is the best way of coming to know about God, and it certainly would not appear to be the only way. The religious believer typically comes to believe in God as a result of or in the process of coming to believe in Christianity or some other theistic religion. (In what follows I will take Christianity as an example of a theistic religion. I will drop the cumbersome phrase "or some other theistic religion," but it is implied nonetheless.) He may come to believe in God by accepting Jesus as one who reveals God. He does not have to first believe in God and then afterward become a Christian. The two may occur simultaneously, and logically the reasons for thinking that theism is true may be the reasons for thinking Christianity is true.

It is not evident, then, that the success of natural theology is crucial to religious belief. Many Christian theologians, especially Protestants, have actually been hostile to natural theology. Such hostility may stem from the kind of fideism discussed in chapter one, and indeed I believe that fideism and the rejection of natural theology are often confusedly rolled together. However, a religious believer could reject natural theology without being a fideist. To avoid fideism it is necessary only for the believer to accept the legitimacy of critical reflection on one's beliefs by analyzing them in light of all the evidence and in comparison with alternative views. It is not required that one abstract a "core," such as theism, from a total set of beliefs, such as Christianity, to be considered in isolation.

Actually the distinction between natural theology and revealed theology is not so easy to make as one might think. The believer who rejects natural theology usually claims to know about God because he has experienced God or because God has revealed himself, either directly or through special people, events and/or sacred writings, often accompanied by miracles or other special signs. It would seem possible to regard such experiences and revelations, if they occur, as "natural" evidence for God's existence. And indeed, many natural theologians have developed arguments for God's existence from miracles or from religious experience. In principle, such arguments could be developed without presupposing the truth of any particular religion or religious authority, and they would therefore qualify as natural theology by our definition. If this is sound, then it may imply that the concept of natural theology is not all that clear, and that no sharp line can be drawn between natural theology and other kinds of theology.

Whether or not this is the case, it still seems to me that there is an important initial distinction to be drawn between believing in God on the basis of arguments which take as their starting point general features of nature or human experience, and believing in God on the basis of highly specific experiences or events. Even though the latter kind of evidence can be formulated into arguments, most natural theologians have focused on the former kind of argument. And there is a further significant difference. The natural theologian who begins from general features of nature usually aims to arrive only at that subset of religious beliefs called theism. The person who believes in God on the basis of a historical revelation accompanied by miracles is much more likely to accept theism only as a part of a more inclusive set of beliefs.

In any case we shall proceed in the remainder of this chapter and in the next chapter to look at natural theology in the traditional sense of arguments for God's existence which appeal to general features of human experience. Then in chapter four we shall look at religious experiences and other proposed "particular" means of coming to know about God.

Proofs of God's Existence

One way the project of natural theology has been formulated is in the question of whether God's existence can be *proved*. Many philosophers have developed arguments which purport to be such proofs; many others have attempted to find flaws in these arguments.

Before attempting to explain some of these arguments and evaluate their success as proofs, it is necessary to say something about arguments and how they might be judged successful. Philosophers usually think of an argument as a set of statements or propositions (the premises) which show that another statement (the conclusion) is true or which increase the probability that the conclusion is true. Arguments can be either deductive or inductive. A good deductive argument is an argument in which the premises *entail* the conclusion; the conclusion cannot be false if the premises are true. A good inductive argument is one in which the premises make the conclusion more likely to be true. Most arguments given by philosophers for the existence of God have been deductive arguments, although some important twentieth-century philosophers have put forward inductive arguments.

In his book *Belief in God*, George Mavrodes outlines four ways of assessing the value of deductive arguments.[2] These four ways give us four questions that can be asked about an argument: Is it valid? Is it sound? Is it cogent? Is it convincing?

Validity is a term used by logicians in evaluating the formal structure of an argument. An argument is valid when the conclusion must be true if the premises are true. The following is an example of a valid argument.

1. All people from Georgia always speak with a Southern accent.

2. C. Stephen Evans is from Georgia.

3. Therefore, C. Stephen Evans always speaks with a Southern accent.

Although this argument is valid, the conclusion is false, since C. Stephen Evans rarely speaks with a Southern accent. The argument is valid because the conclusion would be true *if* the premises were true. But in this case premise 1 is false.

An argument is *sound* if it is valid *and* all the premises of the argument are true. If an argument is sound, then its conclusion is true. Presumably those who want to prove God's existence will want, as a minimum, arguments which are sound.

It would seem clear, however, that the logical criteria of validity and soundness are not enough to characterize a successful proof of God's existence. It is possible for an argument to be sound (valid with true premises) without anyone's knowing it to be sound. A sound argument for God's existence will not be valuable unless it can be known to be sound. Mavrodes defines a *cogent* argument as one which is both sound and known by someone to be sound.

Adding cogency to our list of evaluative criteria complicates matters enormously because of the reference in the definition to "someone." Which arguments are cogent depends in part on people and what people know. We must ask not simply whether an argument is cogent but whether it is cogent for a certain person or type of person.

One might think that cogency would be all that one could ask of an argument, but this is not the case. Mavrodes gives the following kind of example of an argument which is cogent to most people but is nevertheless fairly worthless as an argument.[3]

1. Either Jupiter has no satellite or Reagan is a Republican.
2. Jupiter has a satellite.
3. Therefore, Reagan is a Republican.

This argument is logically valid. Any argument of the form

$$\frac{\begin{array}{c} \textit{Either p or q} \\ \textit{Not p} \end{array}}{\textit{Therefore q}}$$

is valid, and this argument can be reduced to that form. Furthermore, the argument is sound. Both of its premises are true. (Premise 1 is true because a disjunctive proposition is true if either of its disjuncts are true.) Furthermore, the argument is cogent, at least for most people, since most people know the premises are true and can recognize that the argument is valid. Nevertheless, to say the least, the argument is not inspiring.

The defect which it undoubtedly possesses suggests a fourth criterion for evaluating an argument. A useful argument is not only known to be cogent, but it is known to be cogent in a certain manner. In the argument above, the first premise is known to be true because it is already known that Reagan is a Republican, which is the conclusion of the argument. Although it is conceivable that someone could know premise 1 without already knowing the conclusion, it seems unlikely. What one would like from an argument is that the argument be known to be cogent on grounds *independent* of the conclusion. Only in this way could an argument ever change someone's mind or add

conviction to an already-held opinion. If an argument is cogent
and can be known to be cogent by someone on grounds which
are independent of the conclusion of the argument, Mavrodes
terms the argument *convincing*. It seems to me that one should
say such an argument is more than convincing; it is *rationally
convincing*, and I shall use that term. Obviously whether an
argument is rationally convincing, like its being cogent, will be
relative to people and the knowledge they possess. In Mavrodes'
terminology, the concept is in part "person-relative."[4]

It would seem reasonable to say that an argument will be a
successful proof only if it is rationally convincing in the above
sense. But since being rationally convincing is person-relative, it
follows that a proof will also be relative to persons. Whether an
argument is a successful proof depends not only on whether the
argument is logically sound, but also on whether, how and by
whom the argument is known to be sound.

To whom should an argument be rationally convincing if it
is to be a successful proof? An argument rationally convincing
to even one person would possibly be valuable to that person.
If this definition of a proof is adopted, then it seems plausible
to claim that God's existence can indeed be proven, for reasons
that will emerge in the next chapter.

Many philosophers would not be happy with such a definition
of a proof, however. They have been troubled by the thought
that individuals are often mistaken in their beliefs. If one and
only one person claimed to find an argument for God's existence
rationally convincing, but nobody else found that argument
rationally convincing, surely it is probable that the individual is
mistaken. These philosophers want to claim that a genuine proof
should be rationally convincing to everyone, or at least to all sane
and rational people who have had opportunity to consider the
argument. If we define a proof of God's existence as an
argument which is rationally convincing to all sane, rational
people, then I shall argue that no proofs of God's existence can

be given.

This conclusion is neither exciting nor disturbing, however, for anyone who has rejected neutralism. Even if the arguments fail as proofs, they may succeed in other ways and have other functions. Furthermore, the claim that to know something one must be able to prove it in the second sense of proof is one which carries an implicit commitment to neutralism, for, in effect, one is being asked to adopt a totally disinterested standpoint, accepting only those truths which all sane, rational people would accept. It seems unlikely to me (for reasons given in chapter one) that any interesting things can be known or proved in this manner. Hence the failure to produce a proof of God's existence does not necessarily mean that no one has any knowledge of God. Nor does it necessarily mean that no one arrives at such knowledge by rationally convincing arguments. We will consider the possibility of this in the next chapter as we examine some specific arguments.

3

Classical Arguments
for God's Existence

*M*any different arguments for God's existence have been put forward. Most of them fall into a relatively small number of groups or families. We shall consider four of the most important classes of arguments: ontological, cosmological, teleological and moral.

It is important to recognize that there is no such thing as *the* cosmological argument or *the* teleological argument, although many philosophers have mistakenly assumed this to be the case. Many different versions of each of these arguments have been proposed, and some differ radically from others in the same category. For this reason alone one should be wary of claims to have given a final refutation of one of these types of arguments. It would be difficult to show that an objection applies to *all forms* of an argument and even more difficult to show that no one will ever invent a version of the argument to which the objection does not apply.

In the following discussions I will suggest the variety of versions possible for each type. It is impossible obviously, to give a careful review of all the arguments which have been proposed or to list all the objections which have been raised. So in each case I will, after some general comments about the "family" of argument, consider one relatively simply version of the argument which is clearly logically valid. Then I will consider whether this argument could be rationally convincing to anyone. But of course even if the specific argument I consider fails to convince, this does not prove that every argument of that type would fail.

Ontological Arguments

Ontological arguments attempt to show that the very concept or idea of God implies his reality. If a person can clearly conceive of God, then he or she ought to be able to understand that God must exist. Credit for first formulating this argument is usually given to St. Anselm, eleventh-century archbishop of Canterbury. Various versions of the argument have been defended by such famous philosophers as Descartes and Leibniz. The twentieth century has seen a great revival of interest in the argument, with thinkers such as Charles Hartshorne, Norman Malcolm and Alvin Plantinga defending it.

Anselm's original version is developed in his *Proslogion* in the course of some reflections on "the fool who hath said in his heart, There is no God."[1] Anselm reasons that even to deny God's existence the fool must understand the idea of God. God must exist at least as an idea in the understanding of the fool. What is the idea of God? To Anselm God is the greatest possible being, "a being than which none greater can be conceived."

Anselm claims that it is greater or better to exist in reality than merely to exist in the understanding. Since God is by definition the greatest possible being, says Anselm, it is impossible for God to exist *only* in the understanding of the fool. For in that case a greater being than God could easily be conceived, namely, a being that exists both in understanding *and* in reality. Put into numbered steps the argument goes something like this:

1. God is the greatest possible being.
2. God exists at least in the mind or understanding.
3. A being who exists only in the mind is not so great as a being who exists in reality as well as in the mind.
4. If God existed only in the mind, he would not be the greatest possible being.
5. Hence God must exist in reality as well as in the mind.

As might be expected, this argument has met with many objections, for the claim that the existence of something can be inferred merely from its definition is implausible to most people. Gaunilo, a contemporary of Anselm, produced a parody of the argument which attempted to prove that a perfect island—"an island than which none greater can be conceived"—must exist. Anselm's reply to this was essentially that the concept of God is a unique one. God, unlike islands and other finite objects, is a *necessary* being. The implication is that the concept of a "greatest or most perfect possible island" may not be coherent. Perhaps for any island we conceive, we could always conceive a more perfect one. But only a necessary being can be a greatest possible being. The significance of Anselm's reply will be made evident below.

A famous objection made by Kant and others is that one cannot legitimately think of "existence" as a property which an entity may or may not have or may have in varying degrees. To say of something that it exists is not to say that it has some property like "being red," but that the entity in question, with all its properties, has been actualized. When we think of an object, we always implicitly think of it as existing. But if existence is not a property, then it cannot be a property that adds to God's greatness, which is required by the argument. The debate whether existence is a property (or whether "exists" is a proper predicate) is not one we can here resolve, though it does seem safe to claim that existence is no *ordinary* property.

Another popular objection is the claim that Anselm's argument tells us only about the definition of God; it cannot tell us whether anything satisfies that definition. Anselm tells us, quite properly, that when we think of God we think of him as a real being, even as a necessarily real being, a being who cannot fail to exist. Such a definition, however, like all definitions, only tells us what God would be like *if* he existed. It cannot establish the fact *that* he exists.

Contemporary versions of the argument have focused on the concept of necessary existence, which Anselm employed in his reply to Gaunilo and in chapter three of his *Proslogion*. Some philosophers, such as Norman Malcolm, have actually claimed that Anselm developed two arguments. The first emphasized existence as a "great-making property," which Malcolm thinks is fallacious since existence is not a property at all. The second posited the concept of necessary existence.[2] The gist of the second argument, as Malcolm formulates it, is as follows: God is by definition a being who does not merely happen to exist. God can neither come into existence nor pass out of existence, since a being who could do either simply would not be God. It follows from this that if God exists at all, then his existence is necessary. If he does not exist, then his existence is impossible. But either God exists or he does not exist, so God's existence is either necessary or impossible. Since it does not seem plausible to say that God's existence is impossible, then it follows that his existence is necessary. So if God's existence is possible, then it is necessary. More formally the argument can be put like this:

1. If God exists, his existence is necessary.
2. If God does not exist, his existence is impossible.
3. Either God exists or he does not exist.
4. God's existence is either necessary or impossible.
5. God's existence is possible (not impossible).
6. Therefore God's existence is necessary.

How shall we evaluate this argument? Is it formally valid? It certainly appears to be. Is it sound? To be sound the premises must be true. Of the five premises the one most troubling is number 5.

How do we know that God's existence is really possible? The premise appears innocuous enough; it seems as if we were saying simply that there might be a God. It turns out to be a rather powerful claim, however, since God's existence is only possible if it is necessary. Why should not the atheist reject 5 and claim that God's existence, when the matter is fully understood, can be seen to be impossible? Since God does not exist, it is not possible that he ever has or ever will.

On the other hand, anyone who believes that God actually exists will have to judge that this premise is true and that therefore the argument is sound. For the *possibility* of God's existence surely follows from the actuality of his existence. Still we should recall that a successful proof must be more than merely sound. It must be rationally convincing. Here the argument seems to fail, for it is hard to see why an atheist should not reject premise 5 and steadfastly maintain the impossibility of God's existence. And even though theists will judge the argument sound and it will therefore be for them cogent, it will not be rationally convincing to them either unless they can somehow *know* that God's existence is possible *without* inferring it from his actual existence. We must recall that, for an argument to be rationally convincing for someone, the premises must be known to that person on grounds independent of the conclusion.

Even if the argument fails as a rationally convincing proof, however, it may still accomplish other tasks. Alvin Plantinga, a defender of a contemporary version of the ontological argument, asserts that, although the argument may not be a proof, it does show that it is reasonable to believe in God. The key premise, that God's existence is possible, although it may not be known, is a proposition which could reasonably be accepted: the

argument shows the "rational acceptability" of theism.[3] This
seems sound, but it should be noted that the atheist can perhaps
make a similar claim: it is not clearly contrary to reason to assert
that God's existence is impossible.

Karl Barth interprets Anselm's argument not as a proof but
as an attempt to understand more deeply what is accepted by
faith.[4] It does seem very plausible that Anselm's purposes in
putting forward this argument may be very different from those
of contemporary philosophers who have defended the argument.
In any case, regardless of the value of the ontological argument
as a proof, reflection on it does deepen our appreciation of God
as a necessary being.

The argument also serves the function of "smoking out" the
atheist. If the argument is valid, then the person who wishes to
deny that God exists must claim that God's existence is impossible. That may be a stronger claim than the person may initially
have wished to make. This last point can be generalized into a
moral which can be applied to all the theistic arguments. The
arguments can be rejected, but the person who rejects them pays
a price. For to deny a proposition is logically equivalent to
asserting another proposition. To deny p is to assert not-p. In
some cases the assertions required to reject theistic arguments
may be troublesome ones.

Cosmological Arguments

Cosmological arguments are, as the name implies, attempts to
infer the existence of God from the existence of the cosmos or
universe. Such arguments may take as their starting point the
existence of the universe as a whole, of particular objects, or of
even one individual object. These arguments are sometimes
called first-cause arguments because they attempt to infer that
God must exist as the first or ultimate cause of the universe.[5]

The historical roots of this argument go back to the Greek
philosophers Plato and Aristotle, but it was more fully devel-

oped in the medieval period by Thomas Aquinas and Duns Scotus. Of the five arguments for God's existence given by Thomas Aquinas in his *Summa Theologica*, the first three appear to be versions of the cosmological argument. Later on Samuel Clarke and Leibniz defended their own versions, and in the twentieth century the argument has been defended by Richard Taylor. Richard Swinburne defends the argument in a somewhat novel way by treating it as an inductive argument, or probability argument, rather than a strictly deductive argument.

We have already noted a distinction between versions which take as a premise the existence of the universe as a whole and those which take as their starting point the existence of some part of the universe. These we will term whole and part arguments, respectively. In addition to this, it is important to distinguish between versions of the argument which presuppose that the universe had a beginning in time and those which do not. The former versions we will call temporal arguments, while the latter we will call nontemporal arguments.

Temporal versions of the argument claim (or assume) that the universe had to have a beginning, a first moment of existence. To explain its existence in that first moment a cause is necessary, and God is inferred as that cause. In these versions God is the "first cause" in a temporal sense. He is the one who began the series of events we call the universe by bringing into existence the initial objects which composed the universe. By itself this argument seems to demand only a deistic conception of God, but someone who holds to it can consistently accept theism by claiming also that God continues to be involved in his creation.

That the universe had a beginning in time has been argued in various ways. Some have claimed that an *actual* infinite temporal series, such as the past would be if the universe is eternal, is impossible.[6] Others have claimed that scientific cosmological theories, such as the big bang theory, are evidence for the universe's having had a beginning.[7]

We shall not pursue these claims further, because the majority of philosophers who have defended the cosmological argument have claimed that it is sound regardless of whether the universe had a beginning. Aquinas, Leibniz, Clarke and Taylor have defended nontemporal versions. They have all claimed that God is the necessary cause of the existence of the universe both now and for as long as the universe has existed, even if it has always existed. God is the reason why there is a universe at all, regardless of whether the universe is young, old or infinitely old.

What is it about the universe that supports the claim that it requires a cause and that its cause must be God? The usual answer hinges on what may be termed the *contingency* of the universe. If we look around us at the universe, each object we see (and all of them taken collectively) appears to be the kind of thing which does exist but could easily not exist. There seems to be no evident reason why the objects of our universe exist, or even why there should be a universe at all. The things we see do not appear to be things which had to exist, things which exist *necessarily*. Rather they are all contingent, things which do exist but might not have. It is then natural to wonder why they exist. What is the cause of their existence? If the cause is something contingent, then its existence will also require an explanation. Ultimately, the explanation of contingent beings' existence will be incomplete unless there exists a *necessary* being, a being which cannot fail to exist, who is the cause of the existence of all contingent beings. Only such a necessary being will fail to require some further explanation. We can formalize the key elements in this argument as follows:

1. Some contingent beings exist.
2. If any contingent beings exist, then a necessary being must exist (because contingent beings require a necessary being as their ultimate cause).
3. Therefore there exists a necessary being (which is the ultimate cause of the existence of contingent beings).

If we are willing to define *God* as "a necessary being who is the cause of the existence of contingent beings," then the argument, if successful, is a proof of God's existence.

Once more the argument appears to be formally valid, so the interesting questions are whether it is sound and rationally convincing. Before attempting to decide these questions, however, I wish to first deal with three common and popular objections to the argument. These objections may have force against some versions of the argument, but they are irrelevant with respect to the argument we are considering. Pointing this out will bring into focus the real issues.

Objection 1. The universe might always have existed. *Reply:* This objection applies only to temporal versions of the argument. Our version does not assume anything about the age of the universe. The thrust of the argument is that the present existence of contingent objects requires that there be a necessary being.

Objection 2. If everything requires a cause, then God also needs a cause. *Reply:* This objection is misguided because the proposition "everything needs a cause" is not a premise of the argument. There is in premise 2 an implicit assumption that all *contingent* beings require a cause of their existence, perhaps even some implicit assumptions about the kind of cause which contingent beings require. But God is not a contingent being. It is not arbitrary to deny that God has a cause, because if God did have a cause he would not be God. As we said in chapter two, only a self-existent or necessary being can be properly thought of as God, and it makes no sense to ask about the cause of such a being.

Objection 3. The argument commits the "fallacy of composition." The existence of each object in the universe can be explained in terms of other objects, and there is no need to explain the existence of the whole. *Reply:* This objection claims that the cosmological argument commits the logical fallacy of inferring that something true of the parts of a whole must be true of the whole. For example, it would be a fallacy to infer that my family as a whole weighs less than two hundred pounds because every individual member of the family weighs less than two hundred pounds. Similarly, the objector claims that even though every individual object in the universe has a cause, we cannot infer that the universe as a whole has a cause. This, however, is irrelevant, since the argument as we have presented it is a "part" argument, not a "whole" argument. It applies to individual objects.

Many versions of the cosmological argument do, of course, begin by claiming that the universe as a whole is contingent and requires a cause. But it is by no means obvious that these "whole" arguments commit a fallacy. Inferences about the composition of a whole from the parts are not always fallacies. One can validly infer from the fact that every state of the United States is in the Northern Hemisphere that the United States as a whole is in the Northern Hemisphere. It is somewhat plausible that, if every object in the universe is contingent, then the universe as a whole is contingent. The mere fact that there are *many* contingent objects in the universe hardly seems to entail that the whole collection would be noncontingent.

With these three irrelevant objections out of the way, we can now consider the soundness of the argument. This is made considerably easier by the fact that the argument has only two premises.

Premise 1 says simply that "some contingent objects exist." To me this seems highly plausible, but it does not seem so to everyone. Some people might want to hold that the matter (or energy) in the universe is eternal. Particular objects come and go, but the matter of which they are composed is, even more than diamonds, forever. So far this is not a real objection to the argument, which is consistent with the eternality of the universe. But suppose someone went further and claimed that the matter of the universe is not only eternal but exists necessarily. It could not have failed to exist. If this person then went on to claim that the only objects which *really* exist are the eternal constituents of matter (whatever those may be), then he would be denying premise 1. He would be saying no contingent beings exist.

Without this last stipulation (that only eternal objects are real) the objection does not strictly undermine the argument, because it still would imply the existence of a necessary reality as the cause of complex contingent beings. However, the cause would in this case be matter itself. Matter would be "a necessary being" and would satisfy the argument's definition of God. In any case someone who thinks of matter as "necessary" thereby implies that at least one of the features of the theistic God is actually a feature of the natural world. It is not so much that God's existence is denied as that the existence of God *as a person distinct from the universe* is being denied. Implicit then in a rejection of premise 1 is something much like a commitment to pantheism. The person who rejects the argument is committed not merely to saying that the material universe always has in fact existed, but that the universe could not possibly fail to exist. A reasonable person can reject the argument by rejecting premise 1, but only at a price. That price is the acceptance of a rival metaphysical perspective that is either pantheistic or close to it.

It seems more likely that contemporary Western critics of the argument would quarrel with premise 2: "If any contingent beings exist, then a necessary being must exist, because a contingent being requires a cause of a certain sort, namely, a necessary being." This assumption is complex and could be denied in two ways. First, someone might just claim that contingent beings don't require a cause at all. Second, someone might claim that though contingent beings require a cause, the causes are in turn contingent. At that point the critic could either repeat the first response (contingent beings don't need causes) or simply claim that there is an infinite series of contingent beings, each of which has another contingent being as its cause. In summary one can reject premise 2 by claiming either that contingent beings have no cause or that there is an infinite series of contingent causes.

The first or "no-cause" objection is essentially a claim that contingent objects have no explanation; they just *exist*. Their existence is what is often called a brute fact. The defender of the argument will claim that it is unreasonable to say that the existence of contingent things is simply a brute fact.

The second response, the "infinite series of causes" view, is somewhat different, since the proponent of this objection claims that each and every contingent thing has a cause—namely, some other contingent thing or set of things. Since the series is infinite, no individual lacks a cause. The proponent of the cosmological argument can deal with this infinite-series view in two ways. First, she might concede that each and every individual contingent object has an explanation, but claim that what has not been explained is the existence of the whole series. Why are there any contingent beings at all? This effectively converts the argument from a "part" argument to a "whole" argument.

The second option for the proponent of the argument is to claim that the explanations of existence offered by the infinite series are defective in some way. An infinite series of contingent causes would necessarily be an incomplete series. An explanation of the existence of each contingent being could also be claimed to be incomplete. Contingent object A exists because of contingent object B, but since B's existence is contingent, it is natural to ask why B exists as well. To the extent that the question is unanswered, one could conclude that A's existence has not been completely explained. This does not mean that the explanation is not complete enough for ordinary, practical purposes, but it does mean that the explanation is in some sense incomplete.

This is why the defender of the cosmological argument finds

the infinite-series view defective. To postulate as an explanation for the existence of a particular contingent object an infinite, incomplete series is really to admit that no final, determinate explanation can be given. If this is correct, then the infinite-series view turns out at bottom to share something in common with the no-cause view. Both claim that the existence of contingent beings has no determinative cause; both therefore entail that there is in the final analysis no complete explanation for the existence of such beings. The proponent of the cosmological argument, on the other hand, clearly accepts what has been called the "principle of sufficient reason." She holds that for every fact there must be a finally adequate explanation. The existence of contingent beings cannot be a brute fact, since such beings do not themselves explain their existence.

The person who denies premise 2 of the argument is simply denying the principle of sufficient reason. He is claiming that contingent objects have no ultimate reason for being; they just *exist*. Once more it is evident that rejection of the argument carries with it a price—namely, the acceptance of a rival metaphysical system. In this case the rival system is naturalism, for naturalism is the view that the natural order exists "on its own." The naturalist rejects the cosmological argument by claiming that the existence of the objects in nature is just a brute fact *ultimately*, though of course provisional and partial explanations of why some beings exist can be given in terms of other finite beings. But no final explanation can be given of why there should be such things as finite beings at all.

If we ask, "Why are there any beings at all?" the naturalist will answer either that there is no reason or that the question is a meaningless one which cannot be answered. Some naturalists have taken the latter position.[8] Others, particularly some of the atheistic existentialists, have taken the former line. Writers such as Sartre and Camus have described the world as *absurd*, meaning that no reason can be given for its existence. The world is the sort of thing which ought to have an explanation, but it does not.[9]

Is the cosmological argument rationally convincing? It may be to some people. Many people have had powerful experiences of what may be called the contingency of things in the universe, including their own existence. Although our familiarity with finite objects may indeed breed contempt, or at least a lack of wonder about them, most people can recall experiences in which they have suddenly become aware of the enormous oddity that anything exists at all—or the oddity that just *these* particular things exist. I am inclined to call these "experiences of cosmic wonder," and I think one's evaluation of the cosmological argument turns heavily on how such experiences are interpreted and evaluated. If one dismisses the experience as meaningless, trivial or neurotic, one will dismiss the question "Why do things exist?" as meaningless, trivial or neurotic. If one accepts the experience as significant, then one will admit that the question posed by the cosmological argument is meaningful. One can meaningfully ask, "Why is there a universe?" Here the debate will turn on whether humans have a right to expect an answer, or whether the universe in some sense *must* make sense. This is, in effect, the question of whether the principle of sufficient reason is true.

I can see no way of disproving the contention of the naturalist that the question has no meaning and cannot be asked, or his alternative contention that it can be asked but not answered, at least to the satisfaction of the naturalist. (One might, of course, try to show that the consequences of rejecting the principle of sufficient reason in other contexts are unacceptable.) Hence, if by proof we mean an argument which is rationally convincing to everyone, the cosmological argument certainly fails. But it does powerfully evoke and articulate the theistic view of the relation which holds between God and contingent beings. And the person who finds the question "Why are there things?"

meaningful and who is willing to claim that there must be a reason why things exist, will find the argument convincing.

Certainly the argument helps us to better understand the nature of theism and how it differs from rival views. It helps us to see that the question of whether God exists is not a question like "Is there a Loch Ness monster?" The question about God is not merely a question about another entity but a question about the character of the universe as a whole. The rejection of the cosmological argument implicitly carries with it a commitment to a rival metaphysical view, such as pantheism or naturalism. Ultimately, the question is not "Can God's existence be proved?" but "Which metaphysical view is most plausible?" A theist may find the argument helpful in coming to the conclusion that theism is indeed a reasonable way of viewing the universe.

It is worth noting how limited a conclusion the cosmological argument reaches. By itself the argument only seems to show the existence of a necessary being which is the cause of the universe. While this does include some key elements of the theistic conception of God, it obviously leaves out quite a few important ones. The conclusion is compatible with many views of God. So, even if it is successful, the cosmological argument hardly constitutes more than an entering wedge into the knowledge of God. If someone accepts the conclusion, the proper attitude for him to adopt is surely a desire to learn more about God. Such a person should show an alert sensitivity about how he may obtain additional knowledge of God.

Teleological Arguments

In a broad sense, a teleological argument is also a cosmological argument: it too begins with the existence of the cosmos. It begins, however, not merely with its existence but with its character as a *cosmos,* an orderly universe. It is often referred to as "the argument from design."

Like the cosmological argument, the teleological argument finds its roots in classical Greece. And it is clearly present in medieval times as the fifth of St. Thomas Aquinas's "Five Ways" to prove God's existence. In terms of popularity, however, the heyday of the argument was the eighteenth and early nineteenth centuries. A particularly famous version was developed by William Paley (1743-1805), an English theologian. In the twentieth century the argument has been defended by Richard Taylor, F. R. Tennant and Richard Swinburne. Tennant and Swinburne, particularly, have developed the argument not as a strict deductive proof but as an attempt to show the *probability* of theism.

The teleological argument begins from the fact that the natural world appears to exhibit purposive order or design and infers that its cause must therefore be an intelligent designer. Aquinas's version of the argument is a good illustration:

The fifth way is taken from the governance of the world. We see things which lack knowledge, such as natural bodies, act for an end, and this is evident from their acting always, or nearly always, in the same way, so as to obtain the best result. Hence it is plain that they achieve their end, not fortuitously, but designedly. Now whatever lacks knowledge cannot move towards an end, unless it be directed by some being endowed with knowledge and intelligence; as the arrow is directed by the archer. Therefore some intelligent being exists by whom all natural things are directed to their end; and this being we call God.[10]

Aquinas here claims that many entities in nature act for an end, or *telos*. He does not give any examples, but it is not hard to do so. Most if not all animals, for example, appear to be self-regulating mechanisms which are designed to maintain their own existence and reproduce themselves. Many of the parts of the animals contribute to this overall goal by realizing some more particular end or goal. Lungs exchange oxygen for carbon dioxide; hearts pump blood throughout the body.

Aquinas mentions two features present in nature which together imply design. The first is *order*. Things in nature "act always or nearly always in the same way." The second feature is *value*. The order in nature brings about results which are clearly good. We shall term this kind of order "beneficial order." Clearly Aquinas thinks that a regular, orderly process which achieves a beneficial result is evidence that one is dealing with intelligent design. Beneficial order, he says, does not occur by chance.

How does Aquinas know this? Why couldn't orderly processes which bring about beneficial results be the result of chance? Contemporary defenders of the argument, such as Richard Taylor and Richard Swinburne, have admitted that it is not logically impossible for these processes to occur by chance. Thus on their view the argument fails as a strict deductive proof. However, although it is perhaps possible for such results to occur by chance, it is, they claim, implausible or improbable. Hence the argument shows the probability or plausibility of theism.

One way (though perhaps not the only way) of defending the crucial claim that it is improbable that beneficial order could be the result of chance is to make an appeal to our experience of analogous entities. Complex machines like watches and cameras show the same kind of complex, beneficial order as do natural objects. We know that these machines are the result of intelligent design, and it is reasonable to conclude that objects in nature which are analogous to these machines are probably to be explained in an analogous manner. Paley's famous argument proceeds in this way, and David Hume's *Dialogues Concerning Natural Religion* gives a well-known statement of the argument in the form of an analogy. Hume also presents many criticisms of the argument, some of which will be considered presently.

It is worth noting that teleological arguments can, like

cosmological arguments, be divided into those which begin with the whole of nature and those which begin with parts of nature. The former attempts to show that nature as a whole must be understood as one teleological system. The latter takes as its starting point the existence of particular teleological systems within nature. The advantage of the "whole" argument is that the conclusion will obviously be the existence of a cause of the whole of nature. The disadvantage is that it is difficult to show that the universe as a whole aims at some end or goal. It may, but it does not seem evident that it does. The "part" type of argument is therefore easier to defend, but it suffers the disadvantage that an inference about the cause of the whole of nature is made on the basis of the character of some parts of nature, which accordingly somewhat reduces the probability of the conclusion.

Let us now formulate some versions of the teleological argument and consider their merits and demerits. The following is a simple version:

1. There exist in nature many examples of beneficial order.
2. Beneficial order is best explained as the result of an intelligent designer.
3. Therefore, nature is probably the result of an intelligent designer.

The conclusion can at best be probable for two reasons: (1) an inference about the whole of nature is being drawn from parts of nature; (2) it does not seem to be certain that beneficial order can only come from intelligence.

Most criticisms of this argument will focus on premise 2. Must we explain the order in the universe as the work of a designer? Alternative formulations of the argument may shift the burden of criticism to other premises. For example, the argument could be put as follows:

1. Nature contains many instances of design.
2. Designed entities are the result of a designer.
3. Therefore, nature is probably the work of a designer.

This formulation makes the second premise virtually tautologous, but now the critic will question premise 1. Is the order in nature genuine design, or is it merely apparent design? The underlying problem remains how one knows that the beneficial order is not simply, in Aquinas's words, "fortuitous."

The analogical versions of the argument, as mentioned, try to confront this problem head-on. For example, we might argue as follows:

1. Objects in nature are analogous to manmade machines.
2. Manmade machines are the result of intelligent design.
3. Analogous effects will have analogous causes.
4. Therefore, objects in nature are the result of something analogous to intelligent design.

As we see from this, the appeal to analogy can generate a self-contained argument. Alternatively, the considerations appealed to here could be employed to back up the debatable second premise in our original argument.

In general, criticisms of teleological arguments can be divided into two groups. The first includes those criticisms which attack the strengths of the argument by claiming that intelligent design is not necessary to explain the order in the universe. The second group of criticisms focuses on the religious worth of the argument. Is the intelligent designer the argument infers identical with the God of theism? Both kinds of criticisms are given classical statements in Hume's *Dialogues Concerning Natural Religion*.

Let us take the former type of attack first. Hume considers the argument mainly in its analogical form; hence many of his criticisms center on the strength of the analogy between the natural order and human machines. First, he claims that other analogies are possible. The universe does resemble a machine in some ways, and machines are at least usually products of intelligence. But the universe also resembles other things—plants, for example, which hatch from seeds and are not the product of intelligence, or animals, which are conceived by sexual reproduction.[11] Hume's argument here is clearly question-begging. In order for it to have force we should have to know already that natural objects such as plants and animals are *not* the result of intelligent design, but that is precisely the question at issue.

Hume also objects that the universe is too singular a phenomenon to form hypotheses about its cause.[12] Since we have no experience of universe making, we have no way of testing alternative hypotheses about its cause. This objection seems to assume that it is not possible to form hypotheses about singular objects. This is clearly a false assumption, however; biologists are always developing hypotheses about the origin of life even though life is, as far as we presently know, a singular phenomenon. In any case we have no experience of the evolution of other life forms, but that is no barrier to scientific attempts to hypothesize about the origins of life. If Hume were right here, then no arguments from analogy would have any value, for he is in effect claiming that we cannot trust an analogy unless we have repeated direct experiences of what we are making an analogical inference about, in this case universes. But if we *had* such direct experience, analogous reasoning would be unnecessary.

Perhaps Hume's most serious objection is his claim that alternative explanations of the order of the universe are possible. Perhaps the order in the universe is somehow inherent in matter.[13] Perhaps the order of the universe is only apparent order, which is in reality the result of mechanical processes.[14] Hume wrote before Darwin, but a Darwinian theory of evolution would appear to be the type of mechanical process he was groping toward. When interpreted naturalistically, Darwinian evolution gives a rival explanation of the order in the universe. The fact that creatures are so well adapted to their environments and that the organs of creatures are mutually coordinated is to be explained as a result of random variations and the "survival of the fittest." A certain amount of random variation occurs in nature. When a variation occurs which gives a creature some edge over its competitors, it will be more likely to survive and pass on to its offspring the favorable change. Given enough time, what appears to be design can be explained mechanistically. Clearly, it is the popularity of evolutionary theory more than anything else which has eroded the credibility of the teleological argument.

To this evolutionary challenge three lines of response are possible. First, some have directly attacked the theory of evolution itself, arguing that creation provides a superior scientific explanation. This is the position of those who have attempted to mandate the teaching of "creation-science" as an alternative to evolution.

A second line of response is to concede that an evolutionary *process* has occurred, but to argue that the process is not one which can be understood or explained purely mechanistically. Chance variation and natural selection are inadequate to explain the order which has evolved. Rather, at least at certain points, it seems more plausible to see the process as one guided by intelligent design.

A third response concedes the validity of Darwinian or Neo-Darwinian theories as *scientific* explanations of the order in the universe, but questions whether some more *ultimate* explanation is not still required. Mechanical explanations and teleological or design explanations are not always incompatible. If a person who desires to achieve some result, say the production of shoes, designs a machine to achieve that result, then two kinds of explanations are possible. One can explain the appearance of the shoes mechanically in terms of the operation of the machine. But of course the machine operates as it does *because* it is a means for achieving the result; it was designed to do so. Hence a more complete explanation of the result in terms of the purpose of the machine's designer is also legitimate. It is not by accident that the machine achieves the beneficial results which it does achieve.

In a similar way, the defender of the teleological argument might claim that the evolutionary process, even if it is a mechanical process, is simply the *means* whereby God, the intelligent designer, realizes his purposes. The evolutionary process, if it does indeed occur, occurs only because the laws of nature operate as they do. These laws are themselves a clear example then of order whose *ultimate* outcome is beneficial order. The defender of the teleological argument can therefore claim that evolution in no way lessens the beneficial order of the universe or the need to explain that order. Rather, evolution simply increases our understanding of the complex and ingenious means whereby the designer-God realizes his purposes.

In evaluating this kind of response, the question which we must ask is whether the basic order of the universe, the natural laws which have operated to bring about the apparent design in nature (if evolution is true), is a brute fact. The critic of the argument will insist that no explanation can be given of why the basic laws of nature operate; they just do. The defender of the argument naturally wonders why we have laws of nature at all, and especially why we have the particular ones which have produced much beneficial order. It seems to him arbitrary and implausible to say that such laws are simply brute facts. Once more, as in the case of the cosmological argument, the person who rejects the argument seems to be placed in the position of arbitrarily stopping the quest for an explanation. He claims that no explanation can be given of something that appears to many to cry out for explanation. I conclude therefore that, although the argument is not conclusive in the sense of being rationally convincing to everyone, it does have considerable force if understood as an attempt to show that the hypothesis of a designer is plausible.

But what about Hume's second set of objections? As we noted

above, Hume also objects to the argument on religious grounds. He says that the argument does not really show that the god of theism exists. The designer of the world might in many ways fail to resemble the God of Christianity, Judaism and Islam. The designer might not be truly omnipotent in power, knowledge or goodness, but limited in various ways.[15] Indeed, says Hume, the designer might be not a single being but a committee.

Richard Swinburne has responded to these objections by claiming that the hypothesis of theism is more probable than the "finite god(s)" Hume considers because theism is simpler.[16] The fact that the laws which bring about the order of the universe seem universal points to one cause rather than many. Swinburne says that it is simpler to hypothesize a God with infinite power and knowledge than a God with great though limited powers. The hypothesis of a *limited* God would inevitably raise the question of why God has just the amount of power and knowledge he does possess, a question which would be unanswerable.

But even if Swinburne is right, Hume's objections do nonetheless diminish the certainty of the conclusion of an argument which was only probable in the beginning. But this simply entails that the teleological argument, like the cosmological argument, is limited in what it conveys about God. A reasonable person who accepted the argument would hardly be content with the knowledge of God thereby gained, but he or she would be eager to learn more about God. Natural theology, even if successful, is not supposed to give the kind of detailed knowledge of God to be gained from possible special revelations and religious experiences.

To a certain extent, however, the defects of the cosmological and teleological arguments cancel each other out. The cosmological argument concludes that a necessary being who is the cause of the universe must exist, but it does not on its face show that this cause must be personal. The teleological argument attempts to show that the cause of the universe must be intelligent and therefore personal, but it does not on its face show that this being must be a necessary being. Clearly, the two arguments complement each other and therefore could be viewed not as separate arguments but as parts of a general case for the plausibility of theism.

Someone might claim, of course, that the conclusions of the two arguments refer to two different beings and that the arguments cannot thus be used together. Here one could reply in the spirit of Swinburne that this seems logically possible but not plausible. It seems far-fetched to suppose that the being responsible for the very existence of the natural order would not also, at least ultimately, be responsible for its special pervasive characteristics.

Nevertheless, if one asks whether the teleological argument is a proof of God's existence, in the sense of being rationally convincing to all, the answer must surely be negative. But perhaps that conclusion merely shows how unrealistic such a concept of proof is.

Moral Arguments

The roots of the moral argument go back, philosophically, to Plato's conviction that the source of all reality and truth must be the "Form of the Good" and, religiously, to the biblical teaching that moral obligations must be understood as divine commands. Although not popular among philosophers, this argument probably is more convincing to ordinary people than any other. The voice of conscience is still regarded by many as the voice of God.

The fact that the argument is not so popular among philosophers as among ordinary people might appear to count strongly against it, but I am not sure this is so. Fashions come and go in philosophy as in any other field, so the fact that an argument is not currently fashionable is not terribly significant. It is plausible to think, however, that *if* there is a God and *if* it is important for human beings to know about him, then God would make it possible for "ordinary people" to know about him. That the moral argument is often convincing to unsophisticated people, while not impressive evidence for its truth, certainly does not count against it.

Kant developed a type of moral argument in the late eighteenth century, but his argument was unusual in several ways.[17] Kant did not claim that the existence of morality was theoretical evidence for the truth of theism, but rather that the situation of a human being who is under moral obligation as a rational, practical being makes it necessary for that person to *postulate* God's existence. The underlying insight seems to be this: it is unreasonable to try to realize moral ideals in the universe if the universe, and the laws whereby results in it are achieved, are indifferent to morality. The rational moral agent must see the universe as the arena for moral endeavor and so must believe that a moral reality lies behind the natural order.

More theoretical versions of the moral argument were popular in the late nineteenth and twentieth centuries. One of the most popular presentations of the argument is found in the apologetic work of the British professor of English C. S. Lewis, who employed the argument in his book *Mere Christianity* and other places.[18]

Like the teleological argument, the moral argument is best construed probabilistically, as a claim that God's existence provides the most probable or plausible explanation of a certain fact, in this case the existence of moral obligations. A single version might go like this:

1. (Probably) unless there is a God, there cannot be objectively binding moral obligations.
2. There are objectively binding moral obligations.
3. Therefore (probably) there is a God.

Many people find the argument unconvincing because they

reject premise 2, claiming that there are no objectively binding moral obligations. Propositions like "a person is obligated to tell the truth even when it does not benefit him" can, of course, be interpreted in a variety of ways. One of the more popular views is that of *cultural relativism,* which interprets moral obligations in terms of social approval and disapproval. Every society approves and disapproves of particular actions, and expresses that approval and disapproval by training the young to think of those actions as "right" or "wrong." Which acts are designated right or wrong differs from culture to culture. Therefore there are no transcendent moral obligations for God to explain. Morality is completely a product of human culture.

Cultural relativism faces some severe problems. First, it may be that the cultural relativist exaggerates the degree of relativism found among different cultures. There are widespread similarities in basic moral beliefs in cultures all over the world. This is particularly true if one recognizes that a great deal of what appears to be moral disagreement may actually be a disagreement about the facts. Two cultures might agree that it would be a bad thing to sell one's soul to Satan to gain power over one's neighbors, but one might believe this is impossible while the other believes that it actually occurs. Hence one does not punish witches while the other does.

Even more basically, it is not clear why the existence of moral disagreements among cultures means that there is no objective moral truth. Culture X may say action A is right, while culture Y might say action A is wrong. Why should one conclude from this that A is objectively neither right nor wrong? Would it not be more usual to infer that one culture is right and the other culture wrong? Or both cultures could be wrong, or both partially right. In any case relativity in moral *beliefs* and practices does not imply that moral *truth* is relative.

The most serious problem with cultural relativism is that it makes it impossible to evaluate cultures morally. Since there is no higher moral standard than culture, one cannot criticize what is approved of in a culture as immoral, even if the culture approves of infanticide, racism or genocide. This view makes the whole idea of moral progress impossible. One moral practice cannot be really better than another unless it is possible for some practices to be truly better than others.

Another popular way of rejecting our second premise is to accept an even more extreme relativism, individual relativism. On this view whatever the individual accepts as right is right for her. A view which is theoretically different but has the same practical result is ethical *emotivism*. The emotivist says that there are no real moral obligations. When a person says that an act is wrong, she is not stating a fact but only expressing her individual emotions or attitude about the act.

It is extremely difficult to hold consistently to any form of relativism or emotivism in practice. It is easy enough to say that there are no real moral obligations; but most people cannot help believing that, when they are wronged by someone else, the act is really wrong. If a person maliciously trips me and then laughs because I have cut my lip, it will seem to me that the person has wronged me and that it is a true fact that he has done so. It is no good to say that the person who tripped me thought the act was right and therefore for him it was right. The act was wrong, and the person should have recognized this and regretted the act, even if he felt no such emotion. The person who did the tripping is likely to say the same thing when *he* is tripped.

So far we have been examining those views which criticize the argument by rejecting premise 2: "There are objectively binding moral obligations." What about premise 1, "(Probably) unless there is a God, there cannot be objectively binding moral obligations"? Some nontheists, such as Sartre, have accepted this premise, agreeing with Ivan in *The Brothers Karamazov* that "if there is no God, then everything is permitted." Sartre agrees that there can be no objective moral obligations without God, and he therefore tries to ground morality in the individual's choice, which would seem to be a form of individual relativism.

Other nontheists, however, are unwilling to concede premise 1. Naturalistic humanism, for example, tries to show that moral obligations can exist even if there is no God. This can be done in two ways: (1) one can claim that the existence of moral obligations is simply an ultimate fact which needs no explanation; (2) one can try to give an alternative explanation for the existence of moral obligations. The latter is the more popular alternative.

It is impossible to survey briefly all the alternative ways naturalists have tried to explain morality, but these are three of the more common views: (1) moral obligations are grounded in self-interest; (2) moral obligations are grounded in natural instinct; and (3) moral obligations can be explained as a result of evolution. We will briefly consider each of those views in turn.

The first view basically boils down to the claim that morality "pays." One should be honest because in the long run it is the "best policy." The reasoning is that if I am cruel or dishonest to others then they will most likely return the favor. Since I do not want this to happen, I must respect what others want. This view faces two major problems. First, it seems that there are at least a few cases where doing my moral duty might require a sacrifice, such as giving my life, which could not possibly result in a net benefit for me (assuming, as the naturalist does, that there is no heaven or hell). So morality does not always pay, even if it usually does. Second, what follows from the "self-interest" view is not that I should always want to be moral but that I should always want to *appear* to be moral to my fellows. When I am sure I can get away with it, there is no reason not to ignore my moral obligations. Some say that morality is grounded not in what pays off for myself but in what is best for all. But that is *part* of morality; it names what is to be explained but does not itself explain. Why am I as an individual obligated to do what is best for all instead of for just myself?

The second naturalistic position attempts to view moral obligations to help other people as based on natural instincts, such as the impulse to feel sympathy for others. Doubtless there are such instincts, but it is hard to see how their existence could be an adequate explanation of morality. For one thing, there are clearly instincts which are, at least usually, bad, and it is hard to see the basis for classifying some instincts as good and others as bad unless there is some higher standard for evaluating instincts. Second, it is questionable whether any instinct is wholly good or bad. Rather it would seem that critical reflection is required to determine whether instincts should be followed in particular cases. In fact, most people seem to experience moral obligations as requiring them frequently to override their strongest instincts.

The third way naturalists try to explain morality is to appeal to evolutionary theory. Human beings who had the peculiar notions that they were "obligated" to be kind, helpful and so on were more likely to survive than their rivals in the process of natural selection. Evolution might in this way explain how people could *believe* they are morally obligated; people who had such beliefs were more likely to survive. But it is hard to see how evolution could explain the fact that a human being is *actually obligated*. In fact, someone who accepted this evolutionary theory could quite consistently reject the existence of actual moral obligations, reducing this view to that of those who attack the other premise in the moral argument.

Generally the heart of the theistic contention is that there would be something very odd about the existence of moral obligations in a naturalistic universe. How, in a world which is ultimately the product of time, chance and material particles, did there come to be such things as moral obligations? Perhaps the strongest response of the naturalist is simply to insist that moral obligations are another brute fact. But it certainly does seem to be an odd kind of brute fact in a *naturalistic* universe.

In what way does God's existence explain the existence of moral obligations? How does it remove or lessen this oddity? Here theists have given a variety of answers. Some have claimed that moral obligations are simply divine commands, so that without God to issue the commands there would be no moral obligations. Such divine-command theories can be developed in two ways. First, one can claim that it is God's commanding an action which makes the action right or morally good. This view is open to the objection that God's commands are then arbitrary; God cannot command us to do what is right *because* it is right. A more defensible position claims that God's commanding an action does not make it right or good, but it makes it *obligatory* for humans. God recognizes what is right and commands us to do it; his commanding us to do it creates an obligation for us to do what is right.[19]

Other theists reject the divine-command theory as an explanation of morality, although they would agree that God commands us to do what is right. But they argue that it is God's nature which explains morality. Morality must somehow be rooted in the nature of things. God is the supreme reality, and he is supremely good and loving; we therefore have an obligation to love and respect him, as well as his creatures, especially those creatures made in his image.

Many other ways of grounding morality in God are possible. All would agree that the existence of moral obligations makes more sense in a universe in which the ultimate reality is a moral Person than it does in a universe where persons are a late and insignificant by-product of impersonal forces. Much of morality is simply a matter of respecting the worth and value of persons, and that seems more reasonable in a universe which is ultimately "personal."

Like the other arguments we have considered, the moral

argument is hardly rationally convincing to all. Obviously we have not shown conclusively that relativism is false or that it is impossible for the naturalist to give an explanation of moral obligations. But once more it seems that the moral argument does have force, at least for those who hold certain views in ethics.

It is also worthy of note that the conclusion of the argument once more complements the conclusion of the cosmological and teleological arguments. A God who provides the basis for moral obligations must be understood as a moral being, a being who cares deeply about the realization of moral values. This is something which could hardly be inferred from the other two arguments.

Conclusions: The Value of Theistic Argument

In looking at these arguments, we have concluded that none of them can be judged to be a successful proof of God's existence in the sense that they are rationally convincing to everyone. Whether the arguments are rationally convincing to someone depends in each case on accepting some key premise or premises which are neither self-evident nor absolutely certain. On the other hand, we have found that there is much to be said for some of these debatable premises and that many people claim to know them to be true or at least see them as more reasonable than the alternatives. It would seem then that such arguments, individually and especially collectively, could form a case for the reasonableness of theism, at least relative to its rivals.

If these conclusions are correct, then this seems to me an important result. However, its importance should not be exaggerated. One huge limitation is that natural theology still leaves us a great deal to learn about God's nature and doings. A person who is content with the meager knowledge of God gained thereby would be a person easily satisfied. A second limitation is that natural theology seems highly theoretical. It seems to lead only to beliefs *about God*, that is, propositional beliefs. On the basis of such arguments one comes only to believe that a God exists, but one does not thereby automatically acquire the kind of personal faith most religions value in speaking of faith *in God* (more about this in chapter eight).

Perhaps, in fact, natural theology is somewhat inferior as a means of discovering God's reality, operating as it does on the level of theoretical inference and hypothesis. Perhaps one would be more likely to gain a living faith in God, as well as a more detailed knowledge of God, if one had some direct experience of God or if God were to reveal himself to humans in some special way. Thomas Aquinas, one of the greatest philosophical champions of natural theology, shares this estimation of the value of natural theology:

> If the only way open to us for the knowledge of God were solely that of the reason, the human race would remain in the blackest shadows of ignorance. For then the knowledge of God, which especially renders men perfect and good, would come to be possessed only by a few, and these few would require a great deal of time in order to reach it.[20]

Thus the limitations of natural theology lead us naturally to a consideration of religious experience and special revelation.

4

Religious Experience

*T*here are lots of ways to approach the reasonableness of theistic belief. One might try to isolate a set of beliefs about God from the more detailed beliefs of the world's religions and consider the merits of these core beliefs independently of the truth of any particular religion. This basically is the project of natural theology. However, it also seems possible for a person to come to believe in God as a result of coming to believe in the truth of Christianity or some other particular religion.

How might this occur? Christianity, Judaism and Islam are all religions which emphasize that human beings, at least some of them, have had experiences of God or special experiences which teach them about God. Prophets and other holy men and women have had encounters with the divine—visions, voices and inspired utterances. To consider this second route to knowing about God, it is therefore necessary to examine the related topics of religious experience and special revelations. We shall do this here and in the following chapter.

Types of Religious Experiences

It is important to recognize that the topic of religious experience is not limited to consideration of exceptional or mystical experiences. Genuine believers in God often feel that they "have dealings with God" continually in their day-to-day lives. Some people seem to experience almost everything "religiously." Daily bread may be received with gratitude as a gift; illness may be perceived as a form of testing or even punishment.

To highlight the way religious conviction can inform the whole of experience, it is helpful to speak of the religious dimension of experience and not only of religious experiences. For some people the religious dimension of experience looms large. Perhaps there is a minor religious dimension to almost everyone's experience. I believe that this religious dimension of experience figures heavily in the classical theistic arguments for God's existence. The person who finds the cosmological argument convincing is the person who experiences the finite objects in the world (and herself) as radically contingent, crying out their dependence on a higher power. The person who finds the teleological argument convincing experiences nature as an orderly, purposeful reality where the good and beauty which are realized are no accident. The person who finds the moral argument convincing is the person who perceives certain situations as placing him under objective obligation and who interprets "being obligated" as a relation between finite persons and a supreme Person.

But in addition to what we have called the religious dimension of experience, there are also special experiences which are properly termed religious. Actually a tremendous variety of diverse experiences are designated as religious. Before any useful analysis of such experiences can be given, some of the different types must be sorted out so that it is reasonably clear what kind of experience one is talking about.

One important distinction is that between the kind of religious experience in which the individual experiences union with the divine and that in which the individual experiences a separation between himself and God. Many people, spontaneously or as a result of long training and discipline, seem to have experiences in which they become aware of a profound unity underlying all things. Sometimes this unity or oneness is seen as total and absolute; the distinctions and differences which are part of ordinary experience drop out or are perceived as less than fully real or even as wholly illusory. This unity is thus regarded as the ultimate reality, what is truly divine. The absolute monist claims that everything at bottom is part of this one reality, particularly one's own soul or consciousness. "That art thou," in the words of the Hindu Upanishads. This experience of union with the divine is seen as revelatory and liberating.

One would expect such experiences to figure prominently in pantheistic or panentheistic religions, and this is correct. Such experiences are not always, however, interpreted monistically or pantheistically. The theist also believes that God is a unitary reality which underlies everything that exists, including the human self. Orthodox theists tend to interpret such experiences as experiences of God, with the proviso that the union between God and other things is never total or absolute. Even within Hinduism there are prominent thinkers who understand God or Brahman as ultimately a personal reality who therefore cannot be absolutely identified with his creatures though he is one with them in a real sense.[1] Other theists interpret the absolute monistic type of experience not as an experience of God but as an awareness of the soul as pure selfhood or consciousness, stripped of all particular qualities.

The experience of union with the divine is sometimes designated as "mystical experience" and contrasted with an experience in which God's separateness or otherness is powerfully brought to the fore. The latter kind of experience is then described as "numinous," to use the term of Rudolf Otto, who gave a classical description of such experiences in his book *The Idea of the Holy*. Others use the term *mysticism* in a broader sense, describing the two types of experiences as monistic mysticism and theistic mysticism.

I must stress that the experience of the numinous does not necessarily exclude any sense of oneness. Although the dominant element in the numinous type of experience is an awareness of God's greatness and one's own insignificance or impurity in relation to God, the numinous experience may also include a sense of one's connectedness with God. Otto himself stresses the ambivalent nature of the experience. God is seen as a reality which is both terrifying and fascinating, the object of desire and of a kind of fear or dread. A classical example is Isaiah's vision of the Lord lifted up, high and mighty, a vision which inspired Isaiah to cry out, "Woe is me! . . . for I am a man of unclean lips" (6:5).

Perhaps we could characterize religious experience in general terms simply as purported awareness of the divine. The typical elements in religious experience are three: a sense of *union* with the divine, a sense of *dependence* on the divine, and a sense of *separateness* from the divine. Pantheistic and monistic mystical experiences emphasize the first of these elements. Theistic experience usually includes all three elements, though one element may be dominant. Thus theists have mystical experiences in which the dominant theme is a sense of oneness with the divine. Theists also have numinous experiences in which the dominant theme is a sense of radical separation from God, who is perceived as a fearsome yet attractive reality.

This distinction is by no means hard and fast. In fact, most "ordinary" theistic religious experiences probably include both mystical and numinous elements, though the "unity" side of the experience is not typically interpreted monistically as an *absolute* unity. Rather the theist claims to enjoy an experienced union with God of the sort which is possible between two persons who are united in love and devotion. But this unity is qualified by an awareness of the great gulf between humans and God, creatures and Creator, as well as the great gulf between sinful creatures and an absolutely *holy* being.

Since our main focus in this book is on the reasonableness of theistic-type religions, I shall concentrate in what follows on theistic-type experiences. The experience of the absolute monist is an exceptionally interesting field of study but also an exceptionally difficult one, especially because the monist so often insists that his experience defies description and analysis. The experience of "oneness" which is so characteristic of mysticism in any case seems to be capable of various interpretations, some of which are compatible with theism. It seems unlikely, then, that the mystical type of experience could be used to justify theism over against its rivals, but it is also unlikely that such experiences could undermine the reasonableness of theistic belief.

In discussing theistic experience, it is helpful to distinguish experiences which are on their face supernatural and miraculous from those which are more ordinary. Many people claim to have seen visions or heard voices which they took to be of God. Others claim to have heard or seen angels, the Virgin Mary or some notable saint. Experiences such as these raise special problems; for now our attention will be on what can be termed ordinary theistic experience.

Two Models for Understanding Experience

Before analyzing theistic experience we need first to get clearer about what it means in general to experience something. The term "experience" is not very precise or clear in ordinary usage. It is sometimes used to designate an episode in which a person is aware of some reality existing independently of himself. "Susan heard the office manager speak" and "Jim saw the foreman walk out the door" are typical examples of experiences in this sense. However, the term "experience" is also used sometimes to designate a psychological process or subjective mental state of a person, which may or may not be caused by anything existing independently of the person. On this usage Jim's experience of seeing the foreman walk out the door consists of a set of visual and auditory images occurring as part of Jim's mental history.

It is crucial to note that, on the second usage of the term, to say that a person has an experience does not imply that what he experiences has any independent reality. Thus, in the case of Jim's "seeing" the foreman, if Jim is having an hallucination, then his experience could be subjectively the same as in a case of normal perception. For "experience" here refers to the "subjective" images and sensations, which may occur without their "objective" counterparts.

Some experiences clearly seem to be subjective in this way. A person may feel sad or depressed without being able to say why. The experience in this case is clearly a mental episode which does not purport to represent any "objective reality." These cases are fairly noncontroversial. The interesting cases are the ones where the person seems to be aware of something existing objectively or independently. His subjective episodes purport to represent some objective reality.

Some philosophers, drawing on the second usage of the term *experience,* have insisted that a person never has a direct encounter or awareness of the external world. Rather, our experience is limited to our own private sensations and images. When a person sees a tree, what he really sees is not the actual tree but a set of images or sensations produced by his brain as a result of the appropriate sensory input. The subjective image then serves as a representation of the actual tree in the physical world. This way of looking at experience we shall term the representational model. The alternative view, which draws on the other sense of "experience" is the model of direct realism. This view claims that in cases of genuine perceptual experience a person is directly aware of what she sees or hears. Thus if the foreman was not present when Jim claimed to see him, then Jim did not really see him at all. Jim *thought* he was seeing the foreman, but he was mistaken. Thus the direct realist model takes it to be the case that if "Jim experiences X" then X must exist.

The direct realist claims that an experience of an object provides evidence of an impressive sort for the object's reality. On the representational model, however, the move from having an experience of an object to belief in the reality of the object is a little more indirect. Since we do not experience the object directly, it is often claimed that a kind of inference is required. The representationalist may reason as follows: "I am having the experience (subjective sensations) I call 'seeing a tree.' Normally these sensations are caused by there being a tree present to me. Therefore, probably there is a tree present to me."

Many analyses of religious experience follow this representational model. Thus, religious experiences are viewed as subjective sensations which occur in the believer. As such the existence of religious experiences is undeniable. The difficult question, however, is to decide what if anything can be inferred from the occurrence of such sensations. Often the argument proceeds in terms of a debate about the cause of such experiences. Take, for example, a conversion experience in which a person feels an intense sense of forgiveness, acceptance and wholeness. That these sensations are really present in the believer no one will deny, but the believer will say that the cause of the feelings is God's activity, while the skeptic will claim that these psychological changes can be explained naturalistically.

It is difficult to see how one could resolve such disputes. The matter is made more complicated in that it is not clear that natural, psychological processes always (or ever) invalidate theistic explanations, since God as the Creator is responsible for natural processes. But it is hard to see how to refute the skeptic who admits no need of any divine cause.

The difficulty in using religious experience to justify religious beliefs on this representational model may, however, be due more to the model and the way it is being employed than to any special problems with religious experience. It is instructive here to look at the results of applying the representational model of experience to other areas. If one consistently holds to a representational view of experience and claims that the knowledge of the external world *always* depends on an inference of some kind, then grave problems appear. For if we are limited to experience of subjective sensations and *never* have any direct awareness of the objective reality which presumably causes those sensations, then how can we infer anything about that reality from the occurrence of the sensations? We have then no way of testing rival hypotheses about the causes of sensations. The only way to avoid skepticism would seem to be to assume that usually the real world is as it appears to be; the causes of our perceptions of objects such as trees and stones are trees and stones. It is hard to see why religious believers attracted to a representational model of experience should not make a similar assumption. What appears to be the activity of God is, normally at least, the activity of God.

To avoid such problems with respect to ordinary perceptual experience, many philosophers are attracted to the model of direct realism. The direct-realist model appears to be a promising one for analyzing theistic experiences as well. Theists often claim to be aware of God's presence, of his love and forgiveness. They may claim to have an awareness of God's providential guidance or of God's holiness or majesty. We shall try now to examine such theistic experiences on a direct-realist model.

Experience of God as Direct and Mediated

The claim that people may have direct experiences of God has often been rejected as impossible, but the reasons commonly advanced for this rejection are not very good ones. Some claim that it is impossible for a finite being to experience an infinite being.[2] Why? Perhaps it is reasonable to claim that a finite being's experience of an infinite being could never be exhaustive or complete, but that is evidently compatible with some kind of genuine awareness. One's own experience need not *be* infinite in order to experience an infinitely powerful being, just as a person can observe a sad person without being sad herself.

Some people claim that the only proper objects of experience are sensory qualities. By "sensory qualities" in this context they mean qualities like being red, yellow or blue, hard or soft, warm or cold—qualities clearly associated with a specific sensory organ. If the proper objects of experience are such sensory qualities, then one might argue that one cannot directly experience God, since it is implausible to regard God as a sensory quality or collection of such qualities.

The doctrine that we can only experience such sensory qualities seems to me a dubious one. In ordinary speech people commonly talk about experiencing things, such as heroic deeds, loving gestures, historically significant artifacts, which are not sensory qualities. The proponent of the doctrine in question must claim that we do not directly experience such things; we experience other things, physical movements, noises and so on, which are *interpreted* as the objects they are. But to this the response can be made that often there is no conscious interpretation going on at all. In fact, it often seems to be the case that one can recognize an object as an object of a particular kind without being able to say what sensory qualities make possible the identification. I may see a woman whom I recognize as my sister without being able to describe precisely or even vaguely the sensory qualities which enable me to distinguish her from a woman with a similar physical appearance. Distinguishing between what is "really experienced" and the interpretation of experience is none too easy.

Even if one manages to draw a clear line between "raw experience" and "interpretation," which seems unlikely, it is not evident that this will be prejudicial to the case for religious experience. Most important experiences which we take as evidence of what the world is like will on this view probably contain an element of interpretation, and the fact that religious experiences also contain an interpretive element will not necessarily make them less reliable than other significant kinds of experience. Most experience is experiencing something *as* something. One must learn to recognize the various kinds of things one can perceive. Perception presupposes the acquisition of certain concepts and skills, so it is not surprising or damaging that religious experience is like that as well.

There is a third objection to the thesis that people might directly experience God, and perhaps it is present as the concealed ground of the first two objections we have considered. It is difficult for some people to understand how an immaterial being like God can be *directly* perceived. They might admit that one could experience something which is an effect of God's activity but not God himself. Suppose, for example, that one heard a voice from the sky saying, "This is the Lord speaking." Surely, one might think that what is directly heard in this case are sound waves which God has caused to occur, not God himself.

To surmount this objection we must make it clear that when we speak of direct experience of something we do not mean that the experience is completely unmediated. The directness is a psychological feature of the experience, and it is compatible with there being a complicated and indirect process which is in some sense responsible for the experience.[3] Much confusion here results from conflating the description of an experience as it is experienced with the causal explanation of what makes the experience possible. When a person gazes out a window and sees a lovely elm tree, the experience may be perfectly direct. No inference or interpretation need be present to consciousness at all. The person just sees the tree and therefore has good reason to believe a tree is there. All this is compatible with a complicated story of how the experience takes place, a story involving light rays and the operations of the eye and the brain. The person sees the tree through the operation of a complex causal chain which constitutes a medium, but he is not necessarily experiencing that medium. He may know nothing about light rays or how the retina and optic nerves function.

In general, then, it is possible to have an experience of something which is psychologically direct but still involves a complex causal process. If one tries to rule out as not being direct any experience involving mediating processes, I suspect that in the end no experience at all would turn out to be direct. It is also noteworthy that human beings are not limited to their own sensory organs as media for perceiving objects. People often perceive things through rather extended media, such as reflecting telescopes and telephones. A person who hears a friend talk over the phone really can hear the friend, even though the medium in this case involves electronic signals transmitted over wires.

Though I would not wish dogmatically to rule out the possibility of an unmediated experience of God—this may be what mystical experience is all about—it seems to me that most experiences which purport to be experiences of God fall into this category of direct, though mediated, experience. Since God, if he exists, is the ultimate cause of the existence of everything in the natural world, it does not seem impossible to experience God through some other object. Nor does the complexity of the causal process thereby imply that the experience cannot be psychologically direct.

Believers in God in any case do commonly describe God's speaking to them *through* the voice of a preacher, or *through* the words of a hymn. They may speak of experiencing God's presence *in* the closeness of a friend's embrace or *in* the beauty of a majestic sunset. God may speak through the words of a sacred book or poem. Such experiences can be psychologically direct; the experiencer may have no awareness at all of making any inference or interpretation. Such cases are plausibly analyzed then as claims to have direct, though mediated, experience of God. The individual takes herself to experience God in and through something else which is experienced.

In his book *Belief in God,* George Mavrodes points out an interesting feature of mediated experiences which seems applicable to religious experience. In cases where extended media are involved, such as in the example of a telephone or reflecting telescope, it is possible for two people to have the same sensory input and yet have two different experiences. A technician who is examining a telescope mirror for flaws may gaze into a telescope and see only a mirror with various reflections. An astronomer may gaze under the same conditions and see an interesting galaxy. The one individual sees the medium; the other sees something else through the medium. What is seen depends in part on the skills and interests of the person looking.

If religious experiences occur which involve a true awareness of God, this phenomenon may partly explain why such experiences are not universally shared. Two people may hear the same sermon, but one hears only the sermon while the other hears God speaking through the sermon. We will discuss next other possible reasons why religious experiences are not universally shared.

Are Religious Experiences Veridical?

Does anyone truly have such direct, mediated experiences of

God? Philosophers call an experience in which the object of experience is being truly perceived a veridical experience. Are any religious experiences of the type we have been discussing veridical? The question is perfectly legitimate because it is evident that not all experiences are veridical. Mistakes, illusions and even hallucinations do occur.

Many philosophers are skeptical of theistic claims to have such direct experiences of God. There are many reasons for such skepticism. One is undoubtedly a conviction on the part of some that God does not exist. Obviously, if God does not exist, veridical experience of him is impossible. But it is hardly fair to dismiss possible evidence for God's existence because of such an a priori conviction.

A more reasonable basis for doubt lies in the alleged failure of religious experiences to be intersubjectively verifiable. Normally we distinguish between veridical and nonveridical experiences by comparing the experiences of various people. If I claim to see a gremlin in my office but none of my colleagues or students can perceive it, the discrepancy is evidence that I am hallucinating, seeing things which don't exist. Public checking procedures can determine whether an experience is veridical. If I am in doubt as to whether there really is a raccoon in my office, I can try to take a picture of the creature; or I can ask others whether they see anything, and what they see.

Critics claim that religious experiences lack this feature of being publicly checkable or intersubjectively verifiable. When Jack hears the voice of God in the words of the preacher, Mary hears only a boring sermon. When Jim feels God's presence as he huddles in the foxhole, his fellow soldier Jerry feels only the cold night air. The failure of others to have the experiences, and the lack of standard checking procedures, tends to undermine the credibility of the experiential claims.

The critic is quite correct here to insist on the importance of intersubjective checks on experiential claims. Some religious believers have denied the need for such checks, claiming that their experiences are in some way infallible or incorrigible. But it is difficult to see how any experience could acquire such a status, and even more difficult to see how this claim could be argued or defended. If one insists too strongly on the infallibility of one's experience, one runs the danger of emptying the experience of objective status. Normally the only experiential claims which come close to being infallible are "subjective" claims about one's own private mental states. If I claim the room is cold, I may be overruled by a thermometer; if I claim it feels cold to me, my claim is hard to dislodge. But the religious believer wants God to be more than subjective feelings.

One might begin to respond to the critic here by noting that, although checking procedures are important, one can only reasonably demand that they be used for experiences which one has reason to doubt. It would not be possible to demand that *every* experience be intersubjectively verified before accepting it, for the process of checking an experience (taking a picture, asking someone else what she saw) itself involves experiences whose reliability must be at least provisionally taken for granted.

Because it only makes sense to check experiences in particular cases, some philosophers accept what has been termed the principle of credulity. The principle of credulity is simply the claim that experience is usually or normally reliable. Things usually are as they appear to be, or at least the fact that an X is experienced provides some evidence that X is real and present. This is far from the claim that experience is infallible; it is rather a claim that experience provides prima-facie evidence which should normally be accepted *unless* we have stronger evidence that leads us to doubt or discount the experience. It is for those cases for which we have reason to doubt our experience that checking procedures are important.

What kinds of evidence can lead us to override or question claims based on experience? Two kinds of challenges are possible. First, one might have good reason for believing the object claimed to be experienced could not have been experienced. For example, if one knew that a unicorn did not exist, that fact would undermine any claim to see a unicorn. Alternatively, one might know that the object was not present to the person, or that the person was not in the appropriate position to have the experience claimed. For example, you would discount the testimony of a person who claimed to see an accident but was in another city at the time of the accident.

The second type of challenge would be an inductive argument which points out that an experience occurred in a situation which in the past has frequently produced delusory or mistaken experiential claims. For example, one would reject visions experienced under the influence of drugs known to create hallucinations.

It is hard to see how a successful challenge of either sort can be made against ordinary theistic experience. Since God is omnipresent, it is hard to see how one could know that a person was not in a position to experience God. Challenges of the second sort are frequently made against mystical experiences, which are alleged to be the product of unusual physical states, such as fasting. It is hard to see how the critic could know that such states are exceptionally likely to produce illusory experiences; but in any case, such objections cannot be made against ordinary theistic experiences which are not associated with any unusual psychological or physiological states.

It seems reasonable to me therefore to take the experiences of theists as prima facie evidence that God is indeed real, following the principle of credulity. However, although it is hard to see how a skeptic could challenge this conclusion, the difficulty in mounting a challenge does not relieve all doubts concerning the validity of such experiences. The theist's case may even appear to be "too easy." The failure of the experiences to be universally shared still makes one suspicious. Regardless of the principle of credulity, it is undeniable that many people doubt whether anyone experiences God. This is especially true of people who lack such experiences themselves, but it is also true of believers, at least sometimes. The question then arises as to how and whether claims to experience God can be checked. Closer consideration of this question may relieve some of the suspicion about religious experiences and establish such experiences as having even more evidential value.

Checking Experiential Claims

The whole business of checking experiential claims is not so easy and straightforward as it might appear to be if we limited our attention to such easy-to-observe objects as trees or books. Even with such simple examples as these it is obvious that certain conditions have to be fulfilled if someone is to check our experience by duplicating it.

Suppose I have observed a book in my office. For some odd reason I question whether the experience is veridical. The failure of my sister, who lives several hundred miles away, to see the book obviously does not pose a threat to the veridicality of my experience. To see the book in my office, a person normally must be in my office. Just as obviously, the book must be there; if one of my colleagues has borrowed it, then a failure to observe it later will not properly count against my original experience. Also the person who hopes to duplicate my experience must have relatively normal eyesight, the light must be tolerably good, and so forth. The person must also be able to recognize a book, which plausibly means that the person must have some understanding of the concept of a book.

To summarize, even in simple cases there are both objective and subjective conditions which must be satisfied for a successful observation to be carried out. Subjectively, the observer must be a qualified observer; she must have the abilities and interests which are necessary. Objectively, the object perceived and the conditions under which it is perceived must also be right. In the case of objects like bacteria seen through a microscope, or wild animals observed by a trained naturalist, these conditions may be very complicated. It may, in fact, be impossible to specify them precisely and completely. Obviously, in such a situation, the failure of someone to reduplicate an experience does not necessarily mean that the original experience was illusory.

The situation with respect to experiencing God seems similarly complicated. The failure of some people to have religious experiences may cast *some* doubt on the reliability of the experiences. But this fact would only be a *decisive* problem if there were some likelihood that the objective and subjective conditions for successful perception have been met.

What are these conditions for religious experiences? It is difficult to say, precisely. Whether a person is a qualified observer in this case may turn on many factors. First, the individual may have to be attentive; he may have to be looking for God. Since we are considering mediated experiences, it is well to recall that in such cases two people with different interests can receive the same sensory input, one perceiving something through the medium and the other seeing only the medium. Second, certain kinds of recognition skills may be necessary; the person may need to be taught how to recognize God's activity. Third, religious people commonly claim that the quality of one's life affects one's ability to see God. Honesty, sincerity and a love for goodness and holiness are often claimed to be important factors.

The importance of these subjective factors is at least part of what is meant by religions, notably Christianity, which emphasize the necessity of faith to know God truly. Most Christians believe that God wants human beings to freely choose to serve and obey him out of love, not out of fear of his power or a desire for selfish rewards. If God's reality were *too* obvious, it would be difficult for even selfish men and women to avoid obeying his laws, for it would be the height of foolishness to challenge an omnipotent, omniscient being. It makes sense therefore that God would make his presence known to people in such a way that those who do not wish to serve and obey him could remain ignorant of his reality. Given the complexity and deviousness of the human psyche, it is difficult to say who is a true seeker after God and therefore difficult to say who is a qualified observer.

It is, if anything, even more difficult to say when the objective conditions for experiencing God have been satisfied. The difficulty is that God is not a passive object to be observed. He is like Aslan in C. S. Lewis's Narnia books; Aslan is "not a tame lion." Things like trees and books just sit there to be seen. People and animals have some initiative. If they do not want to be seen, they can hide and make things difficult for a would-be observer. God, however, being omnipotent and perfectly free, has the greatest possible degree of initiative. It seems impossible that anyone should experience God unless God wills it to occur. And it seems difficult or impossible for us to say when God will do this.

The fact that God must in some sense take the initiative if true awareness of him is to occur is no doubt what leads religious people to talk of the knowledge of God as coming through revelation. If the above remarks are sound, then any veridical experience of God is a revelation, a self-revealing act on God's part.

The skeptic may here retort that God would presumably want everyone to know about himself and should therefore be expected to reveal himself to all. The believer's response to this is that God has revealed himself to all; a general revelation of God is available in nature and conscience. But God, being a particular person and not "being-itself," can also reveal himself selectively and specially. He calls Abraham to a foreign country; he speaks to Moses in the burning bush. God's actions here are to us mysterious, and it would be folly to attempt to specify the conditions under which God will act to reveal himself. On the whole, then, the failure of some people to reduplicate the experiences of religious believers does not count very much against the veridicality of such experiences, because it is not possible to specify the conditions under which a successful observation could be predicted with any degree of certainty.

We have in this discussion been assuming that it is not possible for others to verify experiences of God. But this is surely too strong an assumption. In reality religious believers do not assume that it is impossible for others to reduplicate their experiences. Rather they usually go to great lengths to invite others to share their experiences. They attempt to get other people to assume the proper attitude; they show them "where to look" and teach them to recognize God when he is present. And they are often successful in this: there is a good deal of agreement among religious people about what God is like and under what circumstances he can be discovered.

Indeed, the existence of the community of religious believers who claim to have experience of God provides evidence of God's reality even for those who personally do not have such experiences. A good deal of what humans know is not gained through firsthand experience but through the testimony of others. Why should not this be the case for religious knowledge as well?

5

Special Acts of God: Revelations and Miracles

Since whether a person experiences God will depend partly on whether God wills that to happen, every genuine experience of God is a revelation, a self-revealing act on the part of God. Theologians have traditionally claimed that God has revealed himself in two ways: generally through his creation, but also in particular ways to particular people at particular points in time. The former is general or natural revelation and is the area of concern of natural theology. The latter is referred to as special revelation because here God acts "specially," not merely as he always does. Judaism, Christianity and Islam have always claimed that the teachings of certain prophets or holy people constituted special revelation. When put into written form and invested with special authority, such teachings then become the basis for what is termed revealed theology.

Special Acts

The idea that God reveals himself in such particular ways, while implicit in the account of religious experience given in the last chapter, is by no means uncontroversial. It clearly presupposes a highly personal God, a God capable of authorizing certain people to be prophets or of selecting a certain nation to be a chosen people. For Christians, God's special activity culminates in his actually becoming a particular person in history.

People who find the conception of God as personal too limiting will have difficulty accepting such claims. Although God is not merely "one more being" on the traditional view, he *is* clearly a particular being who has distinctive characteristics and performs particular actions. He does not merely hold the world in being and maintain the laws of nature. To use a commercial metaphor, God's actions are performed not merely at the wholesale level but the retail as well.

The subject of special revelation is essentially an extension of the topic of religious experience. The major difference between this chapter and the last is that in this chapter we will be considering the possibility that some of God's revealing acts could have a particular authority for the believer, and we will give extended consideration to the difficulties involved in believing that God performs "special actions" and the difficulties in recognizing such actions. The latter problem is essentially the problem of whether it is reasonable to believe in miracles and, if so, what miracles it is reasonable to accept.

The topics of special revelations and miracles are connected in a variety of ways. First, on many accounts special revelations of God *are* a type of miracle. It is typical of a believer to claim that the words of the prophets or of holy books were the result of divine inspiration. Such revelations are not seen as events which can be given a completely naturalistic explanation. So if miracles are impossible, at least one concept of special revelation will also be impossible.

Second, miracles usually are a type of special revelation, or at least they can function as such revelations. We will consider various definitions of miracle later, but on some definitions miracles are seen as acts of God which are of evidently divine origin, acts in which God reveals himself in a unique manner.

Third, the writings which are claimed to be special revelations by Judaism, Christianity and Islam contain accounts of many purported miracles. Unless it is reasonable to believe in miracles, it will not be reasonable to think that these revelations are completely trustworthy. It will be necessary to "demythologize them."

Fourth, since few people have personal experience of miracles, the evidential relation may also go the other way. The evidence for miracles may consist chiefly in the testimony of a special revelation. The reasonableness of belief in at least specific miracles may then depend on the reasonableness of regarding a revelation as having special authority.

We shall begin by considering various views of revelation, some of which attempt to interpret revelation such that its "miraculous" character is eliminated or made unnecessary. After criticism of some of these rival views we shall return to a "traditional" view and then further explore the general problem of miracles.

Theories of Revelation

Within the Christian tradition three major views of revelation have emerged. These views have counterparts in other religions as well. Hence, although the following focuses on the problems of revelation as they have been faced by Christians, the discussion has relevance to followers of other religions as well since these other believers face analogous problems. Such a brief account as will be given here will require overgeneralization and simplification. Each of the three views is capable of more varied and subtle development than this exposition can show.

The traditional view. The traditional Christian view of revelation, one still held by many conservative Catholics and Protestants, is that the Bible is the authoritative revelation of God to humanity. (Catholics differ from Protestants in emphasizing the authoritative revelation embodied in the traditional teachings of the church as well.) The Bible is here understood as a source of truth about God, revealing that he exists, what he is like, and what he has done in relation to human beings.

The traditional view is often called the *propositional* view because of its emphasis on the Bible as a source of propositional truths. This view is easily caricatured. Not only enemies have done so; sometimes its friends have caricatured it by taking it to an extreme position. Thus some have taken the propositional view as the claim that divine revelation consists *exclusively* of propositions. The Bible has sometimes been seen as a textbook or encyclopedia, a handy source of truth on any field.

Such extreme views must be seen as aberrations, not as the mainstream traditional position. Christians have historically believed that God revealed himself in history through his *actions*. He revealed himself to such men as Abraham and Moses by calling them to specific tasks. Later God spoke through judges and prophets, finally culminating his revelatory actions by actually becoming a human being. Jesus' life, death and resurrection, and the interpretation given of these by the apostles Jesus selected and commissioned, are God's consummating revelatory deeds. All these actions can, of course, be described in propositions, but that does not mean the actions are themselves propositions. The emphasis on the Bible as revelation follows naturally from the belief that the Bible is a divinely inspired record and interpretation of these revelatory actions. Apart from the Bible, human beings would have little knowledge or understanding of God's revelatory actions.

The intent of the propositional view is not then to deny that God reveals himself in *actions*, but to emphasize the fact that one of God's revelatory actions is *speaking* to human beings through divinely inspired human authors. Nor of course is the propositional truth conveyed by the Bible simply presented as a set of facts to be intellectually accepted. The truths include teachings about the human condition and relation to God and about the kind of response to the revelation which God demands. Such truths are only properly accepted when acted on.

The special authority of the Bible is often expressed in the claim that it was written by the inspiration of God. Although the authors were human and their own human characteristics are embodied in the writings, the content of what they wrote was guided by God himself. The writing of the Bible was itself a kind of miracle—a special act of God. The Bible is then "the final authority in matters of faith and practice." Some understand this authority to imply that the Scriptures must be *inerrant* in all matters, including history and science. Others believe that the authority of the Scriptures does not extend to these areas because God did not intend to teach humans in these areas through the Bible. Despite such disagreements, proponents of the traditional view are agreed that the Bible is itself the Word of God, an authoritative revelation which can be trusted to give us the truth about humans and God.

The liberal view. The view of revelation associated with classical liberal theology of the nineteenth century has its sources in two eighteenth-century developments. The first is what is often termed Enlightenment rationalism. This philosophical mindset which developed in the eighteenth century emphasized the use of reason to discover truth. The Enlightenment thinkers took reason as contrasting with the blind faith in authority which they believed to be characteristic of the Middle Ages. Kant expressed the spirit of the Enlightenment nicely in a well-known essay in which he claimed that to be truly enlightened is "to dare to use your own reason."[1] The spirit of the Enlightenment was hostile to the claim that a particular historical book could have special

authority over the individual. The world view of the Enlightenment was also not favorable to miracles and other special acts
of God. As scientific knowledge of the laws of nature developed,
belief in miracles and the like was regarded as superstition.

The second important factor in the development of the
classical liberal view of revelation was the growth of "higher-
criticism." Biblical scholars began to investigate the Scriptures
in the same way they looked at other classical texts. They put
forth historical and literary hypotheses, claiming for example
that the Pentateuch, instead of being the work of a single divinely inspired author, reflected the work of many different people
over a long period of time. Prophecies which seemed to have
been miraculously fulfilled were said to have been written after
the fulfilling events. Stories of miracles were regarded as inter-
polations added by pious commentators at a later date, not eye-
witness reports.

How did philosophical rationalism and biblical criticism
interact? Clearly, the higher biblical criticism provided much
impetus for challenging the traditional view of the Bible as a
special, revelatory set of documents. By undermining scriptural
authority, it strengthened the position of those who were
skeptical of miracles and other special acts of God. However,
biblical critics often borrowed philosophical assumptions which
affected their historical-literary findings. The two movements
reinforced one another, and it is probably not possible to say
which caused which.

The upshot of all this is a view of the Bible as a purely human
book, a unique record of the evolving religious consciousness of
the Jewish people. The Jewish people had unique religious
sensitivities; they were a people of religious genius, just as the
Greeks were a people of philosophical and artistic genius.
Present in the biblical record are the experiences of a people
who, beginning from faith in a jealous tribal god, gradually
developed faith in a God of love and justice, a God who is a God

of all people. This revelation culminates in the profound teaching of Jesus, who is viewed as emphasizing the fatherhood of God and the brotherhood of man.

Thus, although the Bible may be an especially valuable resource, it is a fully human book, not one with divine authority. We must critically reflect on the Scriptures in the light of reason and experience. Any authority which it possesses is due to its inherent profundity or truthfulness, but these are characteristics which in the final analysis we must be able to discern and evaluate ourselves.

The nonpropositional view. The nonpropositional view of revelation can be seen as a kind of compromise between the traditional view and the liberal view. This perspective developed as a twentieth-century reaction to liberalism and is often associated with what is termed neo-orthodox theology. However, its proponents claim that the position is consistent with central elements of the theology of the Protestant reformers Luther and Calvin.

The nonpropositional view emphasizes that God is a personal being and that his revealing himself is an encounter with a Person. God does not reveal propositions for our assent; he reveals *himself*. God's self-revelation consists of his saving actions, which were perceived and interpreted by his faithful people. Like the traditional view, the nonpropositional view holds that God has acted in unique and special ways in history. However, like the liberal view, the Bible is seen as fallible since it is only a human witness to that revelation. Jesus is said to be the true Word of God; the Bible is a witness to God's revelation but is not itself revelation, except insofar as God continues to confront human beings through its teachings. God is still a God who encounters his people; thus when the Bible is properly proclaimed, it may *become* the Word of God.

Is the Traditional View Defensible?

If it is not reasonable to believe that God can and does intervene in the natural order, then both the traditional and the nonprop-ositional views of revelation are unacceptable. Both involve the idea of God's performing special revelatory actions. If God does not perform special actions, or if humans cannot recognize such actions, then the liberal view of revelation is the only alternative.

The liberal view, in effect, reduces special revelation to natural revelation. What were formerly called special revelations are simply especially valuable instances of the general knowledge of God made possible by the religious dimension of general experience. While this position may ultimately turn out to be the only one possible for a theist, it would seem a mistake to adopt it without considering whether it is reasonable to believe in special acts of God. If God does perform special revelatory acts, this would be a significant source of information about him. It would be a great disadvantage to be limited to general revelation. It therefore is worthwhile to see what can be said on behalf of the traditional and nonpropositional views. Special revelation should not be abandoned unless it is necessary to do so.

Both the traditional and nonpropositional views involve the philosophical embarrassment (if it is such) of belief in "special acts" of God which are miraculous or quasi-miraculous in character. Philosophically, it is hard to argue for one view or the other. A few points can be made, however, on behalf of the traditional view.

First, it would be a good thing for theology if the traditional view were correct. The task of theology is to gain a true un-derstanding of God and his dealings with us. If God has acted specially in history to give us such an understanding, that is good. Hence it is clearly more desirable that the nonproposition-al view be correct than the liberal view. But for similar reasons it would be even better if the traditional view is correct. For if God has not only acted in history but has also disclosed the meaning of those actions, our position would be even stronger. So it is reasonable not to abandon the traditional view unless one has good reason to do so. It at least deserves serious consideration.

Second, *speaking* is itself a kind of action. If God is a God capable of special actions at all, there is no a priori reason for thinking that speaking to human beings or through human beings would not be in his repertoire of actions. If God does speak to human beings or through human beings, his address must have *content*. One cannot simply speak; one must say something. If God speaks to humans in a revelatory action, it would seem plausible to regard the content of what he says as revelation as well.

Third, many arguments given against the traditional view presuppose false dichotomies. The traditional view is identified with one of its elements, which is then regarded as a mutually exclusive alternative to some other element. A false disjunction is created. For example, it is sometimes urged that what God reveals is not propositions but *himself* as a personal reality. "*Either* God reveals himself *or* he reveals propositions." Now it is certainly true that a personal God is not a set of propositions, and that an encounter with a personal God is not reducible to the acquisition of propositional knowledge. It would be a mistake, however, to conclude from this that the two processes are mutually exclusive. Getting to know someone is not reducible to getting to know things *about* someone, but it certainly may include the latter. In fact, it is plausible to claim that the former process must include or presuppose some of the latter. It is difficult to imagine knowing a person and at the same time knowing nothing about that person.

In a similar way it is sometimes urged that the traditional view leads to an inadequate view of faith. It is urged that faith on the traditional view is simply intellectual acceptance of propositional truth, while true faith is a personal response to God in trust and commitment. "*Either* faith is intellectual assent *or* it is personal trust." Here two responses can be made. First, the criticism foists a caricature on the traditional view of faith. Almost every Christian theologian has affirmed that saving faith is more than intellectual assent. Second, once more a false disjunction is being presented. It must be granted that personal faith is *more* than cognitive assent to doctrine, but it certainly can include assent. Once more, in fact, it can be argued that it must do so. If I believe *in* (trust) a certain political leader, I must also believe some things *about* him.

Proponents of the traditional view can acknowledge that the nonpropositional view is a valuable corrective to what has sometimes been a misplaced emphasis in the traditional view. It should be recognized that God's revelation consists of his *activity*, in which he reveals *himself*, and that man's response to this revelation must include the involvement of the whole person. But there are no good *philosophical* reasons for thinking that such a revelation precludes God's giving man truth to be believed; in fact, there are good reasons for thinking such a revelation would include the communication of content. There is also no good reason to think that personal trust in God somehow rules out belief in that content.

None of this implies that God *has* revealed himself in the way the traditional view supposes. It simply implies that if God reveals himself at all, one could expect the revelation to consist of the kind of thing the traditional view accepts. There are no particular philosophical difficulties present in the traditional view which are avoided by the nonpropositional view.

A further difficulty with the nonpropositional view is the problem of distinguishing the "revelatory events" from the verbal record and interpretation of those events. Logically, of course, an event is certainly distinct from a written record and interpretation of the event. But the particular "saving events" which the nonpropositional view regards as revelation cannot be got at independently of the written records we have of these. Since we have no access to the events other than through the

Scriptures, it is hard to see how one can distinguish the event from its interpretation, at least from our perspective.

The crucial philosophical question seems to me to be whether God can and does perform special acts. If he does, then no *special* philosophical difficulties will be raised by holding to the traditional view. We shall turn our attention then to the question of whether it is reasonable to believe that God performs such actions.

What Is a Miracle?

A special act of God as we are considering it can be understood as an act God performs at a particular place and time, an act distinct from his "normal" activity of sustaining the universe, including its natural processes. To an observer such an act would appear as an intervention from "outside" the system. However, this is a slightly misleading way of describing such an action, since God, as the sustainer of all things, is always involved with and "inside" his creation. Nevertheless this description of a special act of God closely parallels one traditional definition of a miracle.

In his famous essay "Of Miracles," David Hume defines a miracle as a *"transgression of a law of nature by a particular volition of the Deity, or by the interposition of some invisible agent."*[2] Here Hume sensibly leaves open the possibility that a miracle could be performed by any supernatural agent—angels or demons, for example. While the possibility of such miracles is important, we are mainly interested in divine miracles, so I shall in the following discussion for the most part consider a miracle as a special act of God.

It might appear that there could be special acts of God that would not be "transgressions of laws of nature," so that miracles on Hume's definition would merely be one type of special act of God. On reflection, however, it seems evident that any special act of God would be an exception to ordinary natural processes just because it is *special,* though it would not have to deviate obviously from ordinary patterns. If the "laws of nature" are identified with God's normal creative activity, then any special acts would necessarily differ in some way from those natural processes.

Hume's definition of a miracle is often attacked on a variety of grounds. Sometimes the objection is made that miracles are not really violations or transgressions of natural laws. Since these laws are not prescriptive but descriptive, it is misleading to describe God's action in deviating from them on occasion as a violation of a law. A useful point is being made here, and some people are no doubt misled by the connotations of the words *law* and *violation.* However, what Hume and other philosophers mean by a violation of a natural law is simply an exception to the normal processes of nature. This is quite consistent with a descriptive understanding of natural laws.

Another objection to the Humean definition argues that miracles are not really exceptions to the laws of nature. Natural laws describe what will occur given a particular set of initial conditions. When those conditions do not hold, the law is not applicable. When a miracle occurs, however, the initial conditions will necessarily be different since God's special activity will be part of those conditions. Therefore the law has not really been violated.

It is certainly true that something different happens when a miracle occurs. When God steps in "specially," a new factor is added to the situation. But there is no reason to think that the advocates of the Humean definition are ignorant of this fact. The assumption which lies behind this definition is that there are regular processes which bring about results in the natural order. These processes are certainly divine in origin, but they represent God's "constant" activity. When God steps in in a special way, his activity is by definition exceptional in nature, and it is in one sense natural that the effects of God's activity should be exceptional as well. Since God has acted specially, the effects will be somewhat special. No laws are violated in the sense that something irrational has occurred. Still, the events in question will be *different* from the normal course of nature. I see no good reason to quarrel with the definition of a miracle as an exception to the laws of nature which is brought about by a special act of God.

Some theologians, usually those who have already given up belief in miracles in the traditional sense, object to the Humean definition on the grounds that it misses what is really important about a miracle. On this view, miracles are revelatory events, signs—not supernaturally caused exceptions to the usual course of nature. To this it must be responded that in Christianity and other major religions the most important *function* of miracles is indeed that of being signs, events which witness to God's power and character and which provide attestation of the authority of prophets and apostles. However, at least normally, the astounding supernatural quality of the miracles is partly what makes them signs and revelatory events. People in biblical times were quite aware that human beings do not in the normal course of nature rise from the dead. Such "unnatural" events were therefore seen as evidence that God was at work in a special way.

It is possible, of course, for events to function as signs without being miracles in the Humean sense. We have already in our chapter on religious experience discussed how an awareness of God might be mediated through the natural order. If anyone wishes to use the term "miracle" for the broad class of revelatory events or experiences, he is free to do so. In that case miracles in the Humean sense would be a species of the broader class of "miracles." I see no reason to adopt this terminology, however, since the word "sign" can be employed for the broader category of revelatory events.

It is not of course necessary that a special act of God always produce an obvious exception to the laws of nature. Suppose, for

example, that a crucial bolt on an airliner is about to fail, and
that in response to prayers for the safekeeping of those on board
God miraculously fuses the bolt. To all outward appearances the
flight is uneventful; nevertheless the safe arrival of the plane is
a miracle. Such a miracle would be hard to detect and would thus
lack some of the features of miracles which function as signs. On
our definition such an act on God's part would still qualify as
a miracle. Such a possibility provides another reason for not
identifying miracles with signs. Obviously the miracles of a
religion such as Christianity are not mere bizarre events or
stunts. They have a function and purpose, and usually that
function is a revelatory one. But it seems possible for there to
be signs which are not strictly miracles, and miracles which are
not strictly signs.

Is It Reasonable to Believe in Miracles?

Hume, after giving his famous definition of miracles, gives an
equally famous argument against believing in their occurrence.
Actually Hume gives two distinct types of arguments in his
essay. The first is an a priori argument designed to show that no
ordinary evidence would suffice to make belief in a miracle
reasonable. The second argument attempts to show that the
actual evidence put forward on behalf of miracles is pretty weak.
We will consider these two arguments separately. Both of the
arguments are epistemological in character; that is, Hume does
not attempt to prove that miracles are impossible, but rather to
show that we do not or could not have sufficient evidence to
believe that miracles have occurred.

It is perhaps worth pausing to consider why Hume does not
attempt to show in a straightforward way that miracles do not
or could not occur, because it is often claimed that miracles are
in fact impossible. It is sometimes alleged that science has
somehow shown the impossibility of miracles. Even sophisticated philosophers sometimes make such claims.[3] Hume does

not, however, and it is easy to see why he does not. Whether there is a God and, if so, whether he performs any special actions would seem to be, in Hume's terminology, "matters of fact." Hume argues strenuously that whenever we deal with matters of fact, questions of truth must be decided on the basis of experience. We cannot say a priori what kinds of beings there are or how these beings behave. Hume is surely right here, and it would be foolish of him to contradict his own principle by denying the possibility of miracles a priori.

Sometimes it is alleged that miracles are impossible because they are violations of laws of nature. As we have seen, miracles are indeed in one sense violations of laws of nature; but the laws of nature are most plausibly interpreted as descriptive of the actual processes of nature, not as norms which inevitably impose themselves on nature.[4] Whether the uniformities of nature are absolute or admit exceptions would again seem to be a matter of fact which cannot be decided a priori.

Countering Hume's first argument. Let us now examine Hume's first, general argument. This argument presupposes a certain conception of probability and evidence. In his argument Hume assumes that the individual considering his argument has had no firsthand experience of miracles but is forced to rely on testimony. In all cases of testimony one can distinguish between the credibility of the witness and the intrinsic probability of the content of the testimony. Extremely unlikely stories require numerous trustworthy witnesses. Extremely likely stories may be accepted on the basis of flimsy witnesses.

What is the intrinsic probability of a miracle? According to Hume it is extremely low, as low as one could imagine. The probability of an event, he says, is determined by the frequency with which it has been observed to occur. A miracle, as an exception to the laws of nature, must then be the least likely event possible.

A miracle is a violation of the laws of nature; and as a firm and unalterable experience has established these laws, the proof against a miracle, from the very nature of the fact, is as entire as any argument from experience can possibly be imagined.[5]

We will leave aside the question-begging reference to experience as "unalterable," which would contradict Hume's own view of experience. Hume is in effect claiming that miracles are by definition so improbable that even the most impressive testimony would merely balance the counterevidence provided by the improbability of the miracle. Only testimony so strong that its falsehood would itself be more miraculous than the alleged miracle would convince Hume of a miracle.[6]

Hume's argument here seems open to criticism on several counts. First, he does not give adequate consideration to the possibility of firsthand observation of a miracle, short-cutting the problems raised by testimony, although of course other problems could be raised about the reliability of the experience itself. Second, he does not consider the kinds of physical effects or traces which a miracle might leave, which might provide evidence for its occurrence independent of testimony. A healed withered leg stands as evidence apart from the testimony of the one healed. But the most serious defect seems to me to lie in the view of probability which underlies Hume's account.

Hume's view presupposes that the probability of an event is determined straightforwardly by the frequency with which it occurs.[7] This is surely much too wooden and simple a view, and it would create enormous difficulties for the historian, who deals with unique and unrepeatable events all the time. We might take as an example the collision of a planet and a comet. Such events, if they occur at all, are no doubt infrequent and therefore improbable on Hume's view. However, though at any given moment such a collision may be improbable, it does not follow from this that it is improbable that such events have ever occurred or will ever occur. In a similar way a believer in miracles might agree that at any given moment the occurrence of a miracle is improbable, since miracles are unusual events, but he might still claim that the occurrence of miracles at some time or other is far from improbable.

Even an unusual event such as the collision of a comet and a planet may, of course, be highly probable at a given moment. If we know the velocity and orbits of a certain planet and comet, their collision at a certain time may be nearly certain. In this instance we estimate probability on the basis of our knowledge of the actual characteristics of the heavenly bodies, and we do not limit ourselves to our knowledge of the frequency of such events in the past. In a similar way the defender of miracles may claim that whether miracles occur depends largely on whether God exists, what kind of God he is, and what purposes he has. Given enough knowledge of God and his purposes in relation to human history, occurrence of a miracle might be in some situations highly probable, or at least not nearly so improbable as Hume suggests. This is one point where natural theology might make a substantive contribution to religious knowledge. If strong reasons can be given for belief in a personal God, then it might be rash to give too low an estimate of the general probability of a miracle.

In the absence of any firm knowledge about God and his purposes, it would still be rash to claim with Hume that the probability of a miracle is vanishingly small. Rather it would appear more reasonable to conclude that it is hard, if not impossible, to estimate the a priori probability of a miracle; and therefore one should try to look at the evidence for miracles with a somewhat open, though cautiously skeptical, mind.

Countering Hume's second argument. It is at this point that Hume's second type of argument against miracles becomes relevant. Here Hume claims that as a matter of fact the evidence adduced in favor of miracles is pretty weak. Hume points out that the testimony in favor of miracles usually comes from uneducated people who lived in far-off places and times, in "ignorant and barbarous nations."[8] He notes the many forged and false stories of miracles and the human tendency to believe in the exotic and strange, which undermines the credibility of such stories.[9] Also, he claims that the miracles which function as evidence for one religion function as counterevidence for the miracles of other religions.[10]

These specific criticisms are to some extent judgments which must be evaluated by the historian and not the philosopher, and the correctness of such claims must be considered on a case-by-case basis. Certainly not all alleged miracles are equally well attested, and Hume is probably right with respect to the great majority of purported miracles. But it is not at all obvious that his criticisms are powerful against all supposed miracles.

Some of his criticisms seem to presuppose an overly arrogant attitude toward non-Western or "premodern" cultures. In biblical times, for example, contemporary scientific knowledge was obviously lacking, but people knew just as certainly as people today that in the normal course of nature it is not possible for a child to be born of a virgin or for a man to rise from the dead. Hume also seems to be mistaken in assuming that miracles from one religion automatically constitute counterevidence for the miracles of other religions. Even if Hume *were* right here, it would not follow that the evidence for all miracles would be invalidated, for the evidence for the miracles of one religion might be much more impressive than the evidence for miracles in another. It should also be recognized that the "love of the marvelous" Hume cites is balanced by an equally strong skepticism in many people. In general, there seems to be no substitute for careful consideration of specific miracle claims on their own merits.

Contemporary arguments. Some contemporary philosophers have attempted to rule out miracles through a different argument. On this view the laws of nature are defined as descriptive of what happens *always* or *universally.* If an exception to a law of nature occurs, this only shows the law of nature is not a true law of nature, since it did not hold universally. If we knew the true laws of nature, the apparent exception would be seen to be fully natural.[11]

Unless, however, we have a priori knowledge about nature, it is difficult to see how this critic can know that there are laws of nature which would account for the alleged miraculous event. There may not be any laws which hold universally in the strictest sense if God occasionally acts in a special manner. This might seem to create a problem for the defender of miracles. How can he define a miracle as an exception to the laws of nature if there are no such laws? This is not a genuine problem, however. Even if the defender of miracles gives the term "law" to the critic, he can develop a similar concept to describe natural uniformities which always hold *except* when God (or some other supernatural power) operates in a special manner. A miracle can then be defined as an exception to these normal uniformities, which hold generally but not universally.

A second type of contemporary challenge is found in the writings of Patrick Nowell-Smith, who argues that to call an event a miracle is to attempt to *explain* the event, to view it as an effect of God's action. Nowell-Smith claims that a true explanation of an event always involves a reference to a natural law. Since miracles, however, are exceptions to natural laws, and there do not seem to be any relevant laws which describe the behavior of God, then no real explanation has been given.[12]

Nowell-Smith's claim that all explanation requires a reference to laws of nature seems false, however. Historical explanations, as well as explanations of human action generally, are often accepted which involve no reference to any known laws of nature. We explain an act as the doing of a person who had certain purposes and intentions, without knowledge of any natural laws describing what always happens in such a situation.

Such laws may exist, but we neither rely on them nor need to know about them to give explanations of the action. Since theists conceive God as a person, this kind of "personal explanation" provides an obvious analogy to the form of explanation which is implicit in calling an event a miracle.

This analogy provides a basis for recognizing the kind of evidence needed to regard an event as a miracle. The case for regarding some historical event as the work of some particular historical figure depends on the evidence we have for the nature of the event, as well as our knowledge of the character and intentions of the person in question. Particularly important is our ability to place the alleged action in the context of the person's life. In a similar way the religious believer's case for a miracle will depend on such factors as (1) our knowledge of the event (that is, do we have good reason to suppose it is a violation of a law of nature?); (2) our knowledge of God's character and purposes; and (3) our knowledge of God's other actions. By and large the alleged miracles of most religions, especially Christianity, are not freak, isolated occurrences but events which are part of a meaningful context, the story of God's redemptive activity.

Richard Swinburne has developed the concept of a "non-repeatable counter-instance to a law of nature" to describe a miracle.[13] When an event occurs which appears to contravene a law of nature, two options are possible. We can regard the event as evidence for the falsity of the law or as an exception to a law which generally holds. The former is reasonable when there is evidence that the exception is repeatable. This means that if the natural situation were reduplicated, the exception would occur again. In such a case we would probably look for some more fundamental law to explain the deviation. If, however, the exception seems to be a nonrepeatable occurrence, then it would seem irrational to abandon belief in a law of nature which holds in every other case. The apparent exception would be an exception to a genuine law of nature. (There is no compelling reason to use the phrase "law of nature" only to describe laws that hold without exception.)

In certain situations it would appear plausible to regard such "non-repeatable counter-instances" as miracles. Suppose that one had good reason to believe in God and good reason to believe that he sometimes answered prayer. At the very moment that one individual is praying to God for the restoration of the limb of an amputee, a new limb suddenly appears in full view of witnesses. It is hard to see how one could avoid concluding that a miracle had occurred in such a setting.

It seems rash therefore for philosophers or others to claim dogmatically that miracles cannot happen. Miracles seem possible, and it also seems possible for there to be compelling evidence for their occurrence, evidence of the ordinary historical kind. The degree of evidence necessary to have a good basis for belief in a miracle is difficult to determine, however. One's judgment here will be heavily shaped by his view of the likelihood of God's existence and his view of God's nature and purposes. It seems at least possible, however, that a reasonable person could be convinced that miracles have occurred even if he does not have a previously high estimate of the likelihood of God's existence, as long as he is not firmly convinced that God's existence is impossible. Indeed, it seems reasonable that God might reveal much about his character and purposes through miracles. He might show he is a miracle-working kind of God by *doing* some miracles.

Can a Revelation Have Special Authority?
We can now return to the question of whether a special revelation, understood in the traditional sense, is possible. If special revelation is best viewed as a special act of God whereby God confronts human beings and reveals himself to them, then the question at bottom depends on the question of whether miracles are possible. It does seem possible for miracles to occur; so far

as I can see, the type of miracle required for special revelation presents no new difficulties. Such a revelation would therefore seem to be possible, and judgments as to whether such a revelation has actually occurred would basically be made in the same way as judgments as to whether other particular miracles have occurred.

One special problem does present itself, however. If God were to inspire a human being to write a book or utter some word of exhortation, it would not necessarily be obvious that a miracle had occurred. Such a miracle would be in some ways like the hypothetical case of the jetliner discussed earlier. It might appear to observers that a perfectly natural explanation of the author's "inspiration" could be given. Probably it is for this reason that claimants to revelation, such as the Old Testament prophets or Jesus, are alleged to have performed other, more obvious miracles. The obvious miracles have the function of certifying or authenticating the individual's claim to have that special authority which is due to their special inspiration.

Could a reasonable person attribute a special authority to a religious revelation? Often philosophers have seemed to think that the acceptance of such an authority would spell the end of rationality. It is frequently claimed that an individual must choose between revelation and reason, or between authority and reason. As we have viewed revelation, however, it is simply a special class of experiences made possible by God's action. The question of whether a special revelation can be reasonably regarded as having special authority is simply the question of whether certain experiences of certain people could have a special authority in the construction of reasonable beliefs.

All persons recognize the limitations of their own knowledge and experience, and the reasonableness of relying on the authority of someone more knowledgeable. Why should not this be the case with respect to religious knowledge as well? Individuals who have had special revelatory experiences of God would certainly seem to be in a position to have a knowledge of God which would exceed that of people who lack such experiences.

In estimating the reasonableness of accepting such an authority, the key question will be *how* the decision to accept the authority was made. If one regards the authority as vindicated because of its overall value in making sense of the whole of experience, then the decision to accept the authority would seem to be rational.[14] Of course, if one had good reason to think that God were the cause of a revelation, then this would be an important factor in its favor. Here is where the importance of "authenticating miracles" appears. Revelation and reason are not necessarily rival methods of knowing, because it is possible to accept a revelation in a reasonable manner. It is also possible, of course, to accept one in an unreasonable manner. A reasonable person should not regard a revelation as a substitute for thought and reflection, but if he is truly thoughtful and reflective, he will also see that it is not reasonable to rule out the possibility of a revelation on a dogmatic, a priori basis.

6

Objections to Theism:
Modernity, Science and Evil

Many writers approach the question of religious belief today in a thoroughly sociological manner. There is a widespread conviction that we live in an increasingly secularized society and that a trend toward secularization inevitably goes hand in hand with the development of a modern, industrialized society. There is much talk about whether it is possible for "modern man" or "twentieth-century man" to believe in God or other supernatural beings in the traditional sense. For example, theologian Rudolf Bultmann (1884-1976) tells us, "It is impossible to use electric light and the wireless and to avail ourselves of modern medical and surgical discoveries, and at the same time to believe in the New Testament world of spirits and miracles."[1]

Others, such as death-of-God theologian Thomas J. J. Altizer or Bishop John Robinson, have extended Bultmann's perspective on "spirits and miracles" to the very idea of God as a distinct person. Such developments raise for religious belief what might be called the problem of modernity. To use the language of William James, is religious belief a "live option" for educated, reflective people today?

Modernity and Religious Belief

Certainly there has been a decline in the percentage of religious believers in Western industrialized countries, at least among intellectuals and particularly in Western Europe. However, Bultmann's statement that it is *impossible* to use electric lights and believe in spirits and miracles is surely a wild exaggeration. Many sophisticated people do continue to believe in spirits and miracles. Some of these believers are scientists and physicians; some are even philosophers.

Perhaps Bultmann's real point is not a psychological or sociological claim about what it is possible or impossible to believe, but rather a claim that certain features of the modern world, particularly scientific knowledge, make traditional religious belief irrational. If so, the arguments should be put on the table for rational examination. Later in this chapter we will look at some arguments that purport to do this. If scientific knowledge in some way undermines the reasonableness of religious belief, it is crucial to know this. However, glib generalizations about how scientific knowledge is incompatible with religious faith will not do; the specific features of science that count as objections must be explained, and it must be shown just *how* these features make religious belief untenable.

The fact that religious belief has declined among educated people in the twentieth century, if correct, is an interesting fact and no doubt worth some reflection. Many possible explanations of such a fact are plausible, especially given the emotional nature of religious faith and its implications for one's personal life. It would be extremely rash to conclude from such a fact that religious belief is necessarily irrational. And such a sociological fact must be balanced by other interesting sociological facts, such as the amazing persistence of religious faith in China and the Soviet Union, persistence in the face of repeated attempts by totalitarian governments to extinguish it, and the fact that a much higher percentage of Americans are church members today than in the era of the Revolutionary War.

In general, deciding the reasonableness of belief in God on the basis of such sociological facts is like deciding whom to vote for in an election on the basis of who is leading in the public opinion polls. In both cases one has abdicated one's personal responsibility to ascertain what is true or best in favor of the anonymous authority of what existential writers like to call the crowd. Certainly historians and sociologists should continue to explore modernity and its causes and implications, but it is a mistake to think that such studies will answer such basic human questions as whether God exists. Indeed, in the current climate it would seem to be a good thing if theologians and others would cease to utter judgments about what "modern man" *can* believe and think instead more deeply about what modern human beings *should* believe. Such sociological pronouncements are a distraction from the pressing task of examining the serious objections to religious belief that have been made.

These serious objections fall into two major categories: scientific objections, and arguments from the existence of evil. In the remainder of this chapter we will take a serious look at both types of objections.

Do the Natural Sciences Undermine Religious Belief?

In examining the difficulties the sciences allegedly pose for religious belief, it is helpful to distinguish problems stemming from the natural sciences from those stemming from the social sciences. The idea that the development and growth of the natural sciences constitutes a difficulty for the religious believer is rather widespread, despite the fact that many of the greatest natural scientists believe in God. What, exactly, are these difficulties?

Some are hardly worth considering. For example, some purport to find a problem in the vastness of the universe and in the relative spatial insignificance of the earth. It seems hasty to estimate spiritual significance purely on the basis of physical size. The earth may turn out to be a pretty important place when all is said and done. In any case, since most religious believers regard God as the Creator of the whole universe, the immensity of that universe can only add to our impression of the Creator's greatness. It is perfectly consistent with theism to believe that God may have created other beings in other parts of the universe, and, for all we know, God may be just as concerned with such beings as we earth people think he is with us.

A somewhat more troubling problem is the idea that the success of natural science as an *explanation* of the universe has made the "God hypothesis" superfluous or even downright false. On this view theology and science are competing theories which try to explain natural events. The success of natural science then "crowds out" theological explanations. An idea similar to this is prominent in nineteenth-century philosopher and sociologist Auguste Comte's description of the history of science. On Comte's view it is characteristic of a primitive society to give theological explanations of phenomena: "It thunders because Thor throws his hammer." As science matures, such explanations are replaced by mechanistic ones involving natural regularities.

Comte's view is open to challenge on several counts. For one thing, Comte has confused theology with mythology. Thor's hammer seems to be an instance of the latter, and there are great differences between such mythology and the theology of the great world religions. For another, Comte fails to see that *magic* would be a better candidate as historical ancestor of modern science than either mythology or theology. But the most serious objection to Comte is that he misconstrues the nature of a theological explanation.

Though believers have sometimes understood God's activity as an immediate explanation for natural phenomena (particularly in the case of miracles), it does not appear that religion and science usually give competing explanations on the same level for ordinary events. Natural science pushes further and further in its explanatory quest, but the claim that its explanations are ultimate and final does not seem to be a testable scientific claim. Science tries to describe the structures and processes of nature. The question as to whether there is anything more ultimate than nature which explains nature itself, with its processes and structures, is one which cannot be answered by science itself—which is not to say that scientific knowledge might not be relevant in answering such a question.

Theology, on the other hand, is not interested directly in the processes of nature. Theology sees the laws of nature as descriptions of the orderly processes which God instituted and maintains. Theology tries to answer the question of why nature exists at all, and why nature has the orderly characteristics which science investigates. Science and theology do not therefore seem to be essential rivals, because the explanations they offer are not of the same type or on the same level. Science tries to tell us what goes on and how it goes on. Theology tries to tell us why the whole thing goes on and who stands behind it.

This is not to say *particular* theological doctrines could not conflict with *particular* scientific theories. For example, the steady-state cosmological theory, though compatible with theism in general, would appear to conflict with the views of many Christians that the universe had a beginning. (For this reason many Christians are happy that the big bang theory currently has more scientific support.) Such clashes between science and religion seem real possibilities, as they were for Galileo, but they do not appear inevitable. When clashes occur, it would seem possible for the conflicts to be peacefully resolved by one or both parties adjusting their position, as has happened in the past.

The success of the natural sciences has undoubtedly encouraged naturalists to think that nature exists "on its own" and that nothing beyond a scientific explanation is necessary. Whether the naturalist is right here essentially depends on whether it is reasonable to look for an explanation of the contingency of the universe and its beneficial order. These issues were discussed in connection with the cosmological and teleological arguments, and the reader who is interested in pursuing them further should refer back to chapter three.

Objections from the Social Sciences

The sharpest objections to religious belief in our era have come, however, not from the natural sciences but from the social sciences. Although challenges in a number of areas have emerged, probably the most significant have come from psychologist Sigmund Freud and sociologists Emile Durkheim and Karl Marx. We shall look at the sociologists first, and then turn to psychology.

Challenges from sociology. Many sociologists view the gods or God as a product of what one might term the collective imagination of a society. God is a "projection," not a real being. He is created by society for social purposes, such as gaining greater control over individuals. Sociologists see belief in God as providing a focal point for the shared values of a society, particularly those values considered holy.

The particular forms of a sociological theory of religion, of course, reflect the characteristics of particular forms of sociological theory. French sociologist Emile Durkheim stressed the way in which religious belief contributes to the cohesion and harmonious functioning of a society. Karl Marx, on the other hand, seeing society as permeated by conflict and strife, viewed religious belief as related to class conflict. Marx is well known for his claim that religion is the "opium of the people," and he did stress how religion was used by the ruling class to justify the status quo and to pacify the oppressed classes. However, Marx's theory is more complicated than is usually recognized in that he also recognized religion as an implicit protest against the status quo, a longing for a better world which indirectly indicts the actual world.

Now just *how* do such theories constitute an objection to religious belief? On the surface, it is hard to see. Both Durkheim and Marx have given us provocative theories about the social functions which religion fulfills, but it is hard to see how any conclusion about the *truth* of religion can be drawn from this. It is difficult, for example, to find arguments in Marx against the reasonableness of belief in God. Marx seems just to assume that God does not exist, and on that assumption he constructs a theory about why people believe in God. Marx's procedure is typical of sociological critics of religion, who often simply assume answers to the significant philosophical questions about religious belief.

Perhaps the difficulty which sociology poses for religious belief stems from the assumption that a sociological account gives a *complete* explanation of the origin of religious belief, and this makes it possible to explain purported religious experiences and revelations in a purely naturalistic manner.

One must be careful here. It would be fallacious to infer that religious beliefs are false on the basis of an account of their sociological origins. Logicians call this fallacy the genetic fallacy. Strictly speaking, an account of the origins or genesis of a belief implies nothing about the truth or falsity of that belief. A belief which originates in strange or unusual circumstances may still be true; if evidence is offered for a belief, that evidence should be examined and not dismissed merely because of the belief's suspicious parentage. It would seem, then, that the evidence religious believers adduce for their faith should be taken seriously, regardless of whether the origins of those beliefs can be explained in sociological terms. If it turns out that no rational basis for such a belief exists, then a sociological account of why people continue to believe may be in order, but such an account would again presuppose and not establish the unreasonableness of religious belief.

There are strong reasons for thinking that religious beliefs cannot be explained completely in sociological terms. Against Durkheim's theory of God as a symbolization of the power and authority of society, H. H. Farmer has objected that such a theory accounts neither for the universal scope of the teachings of the higher religions, nor for the power religion has to criticize society in a prophetic manner.[2] Against Marx, one can note that, though religious beliefs have often been used to justify social oppression, they have also frequently provided the motivation for those who stood up against oppression—the abolitionists in nineteenth-century America being a good example.

In any case, the fact that religion fulfills certain important functions in society is not surprising and should not be particularly threatening to the believer. Actually, the believer has a great deal to gain from sociological studies of religion. It is extremely important to understand the way social context shapes religion and the way religion influences society.

Freud and the challenge of psychology. A host of psychologists have theorized about the psychological origins and functions of religious belief, but none has been so influential as Sigmund Freud (1856-1939). In his book *The Future of an Illusion,* Freud attempted to explain both the origins of religious ideas and why they have continued to be popular.

Freud's theory, which overlaps sociological theories to some degree, views religious beliefs as fulfilling several deep psychological needs. First, religion helps allay our fears of the uncontrolled order of nature by personifying that order, or at least by viewing nature as under personal control. Second, religion helps us accept the costs of civilization, which Freud sees as taking a toll on our natural biological urges. Religion both sanctifies the rules and institutions of society and promises future rewards which compensate for the pain these restrictions bring us. In our dealings with both nature and society, Freud sees religion as an expression of the longing for a *father figure*. As in the sociological theory, man creates God in his own image to satisfy his own needs. For Freud religion is an illusion, an illusion which produces some positive benefits to be sure, but one which places human beings in an immature, infantile state.

Once more it appears that, even if Freud's account is accepted, it does not follow that religious belief is false. It is not surprising to the religious believer that religion fulfills important psychological functions. If Freud is right, then humans have a deep need to believe in God. But surely the existence of such a need does not show that God does not exist. Indeed, many religious believers would accept Freud's account of the importance of early childhood experiences and the father in developing beliefs about God. For them the human family is a divinely designed institution whose function may be in part to give humans some idea of what God is like and some inclination to believe in him.

Strictly speaking, then, Freud's theories about the origin of religious belief are not objections to religious belief, and to think otherwise is once more to commit the genetic fallacy. It is possible, however, to object to religious belief on the basis of Freud's ideas. (A similar objection can be generated from sociological theories.) One cannot infer the falsity of a belief on the basis of its origin without committing the genetic fallacy. The psychological origins or functions of a belief may, however, provide one with negative evidence if one also has some additional information about those origins. A particular belief held for peculiar psychological reasons may still be true, but if it is known that beliefs held for that kind of reason are usually or generally false, then one has some evidence that the belief in question is false as well.

A Freudian might reason as follows: Religious beliefs are held solely to satisfy deep psychological needs. Beliefs which are held solely to satisfy deep psychological needs are usually false. Therefore, religious beliefs are probably false.

This argument does not seem particularly strong, as both premises are open to question. Religious beliefs do satisfy deep psychological needs, but it is hard to see how one could establish that this is their *sole* basis. Certainly one could not do so without a careful examination of the evidence given in favor of religious belief, something notably lacking from Freud's account. Also it should be noted that religious belief is not always comforting or psychologically reassuring. Many people find religious ideas unsettling and challenging.

The second premise seems even more questionable. People have deep psychological needs to believe in the reality and constancy of the physical world and the reliability of experience as a guide to the future. It would be absurd to question these beliefs because of this psychological fact, even though philosophers in fact find it difficult to justify these beliefs.

The kind of reductionism that characterizes many psychological and sociological accounts of religious beliefs is actually a two-edged sword. Sociologists of knowledge can give accounts of the social origins of atheistic beliefs as well as religious beliefs. If believers sometimes show a deep psychological need to believe in God, nonbelievers sometimes show an equally deep psychological need to reject any authority over them and to assert themselves as their own lords and masters.

The Problem of Evil
Objections to belief in God posed by the occurrence of evil and suffering present a far more serious challenge than do objec-

tions from science. A distinction must be drawn, however, between the problem of evil as a philosophical *objection* to religious belief and the problem as a concerned *question*.

Some philosophers have put forward arguments from evil which purport to show that God does not exist or that belief in God is unreasonable. To such philosophical attacks, philosophical responses seem appropriate. However, many people—believers and nonbelievers—are bothered by evil. When they are faced with suffering on their own part or the part of others, they may pose an agonizing "Why?" A philosophical argument is often the last thing such a person wants to hear; such an argument may appear irritatingly superficial. The person wants compassion and empathy, and the proper response may simply be to listen and try to share the other's grief and questions. At such times the problem of evil calls more for pastoral care than for philosophical debate.

The philosophical problem of evil can be posed briefly and sharply. It appears to many people, believers and nonbelievers alike, that a perfectly good, all-powerful being, if he exists, would not allow the kind of evil and suffering which occurs in our world. Therefore, the existence of this evil seems to count heavily against the existence of God.

The underlying assumption of this argument is our intuition that a good being eliminates evil insofar as it is able to. God, being perfectly good, would presumably want to eliminate all evil; and since God is supposed to be omnipotent, he should be able to do just that. If there were a God, one would not expect to find evil. Since one does find evil, and quite a bit of it, in our world, God must not exist.

The evils in the world which this argument takes as its basis are usually divided (by both theists and atheists) into two types. Moral evil is all the evil which is due to the actions of free, morally responsible beings. Murders, rapes and the hunger caused by social injustice would be examples of moral evil.

Natural or nonmoral evil is all the evil which does not appear to be due to the actions of morally responsible beings, such as the suffering caused by natural disasters and some diseases.

A distinction must also be made between two types of arguments from evil. Some philosophers believe that the existence of evil constitutes a proof that God does not exist. On their view the occurrence of evil and the existence of God are logically incompatible; it is a contradiction to claim that a perfectly good, all-powerful being exists and yet admit that evil occurs. Most philosophers today call this view the *logical form* of the problem of evil.

Other atheistic philosophers make a more modest claim. They are willing to admit that God's existence is logically compatible with the occurrence of evil. In other words, they concede that it is possible that a perfectly good, all-powerful being might have reasons for allowing evil. However, they allege that it is unlikely or improbable that God would do this. Hence, the occurrence of evil, though it does not prove that God does not exist, makes his existence unlikely or improbable. This line of argument is usually referred to as the *evidential form* of the problem of evil.

Theistic responses to these problems can also be divided into two types. The more ambitious type of response is a theodicy, which attempts to *show* that God is justified in allowing evil. A theodicy tries to explain why God actually allows evil; it lays out the reasons why God allows evil and tries to show that those reasons are good ones.

A more modest type of response than a theodicy, dubbed a defense by Alvin Plantinga, tries to argue that God may have reasons for allowing evil that we don't or can't know. The defense does not try to explain why God actually allows evil, but argues that it is reasonable to believe that God has reasons even if we don't know what they are. A defense may give various explanations as *possible* reasons God might allow evil without necessarily claiming that those reasons are God's actual ones.

Certain ways of resolving the problem of evil are not genuine options for the traditional theist. One way is simply to deny the reality of evil, to view evil as an illusion. Such a view still must face the problem of the evil of the illusory belief in evil! Aside from this difficulty, however, such a view is simply not consistent with Christianity, Judaism and Islam, which take evil as something which is all too real and which must be treated with great seriousness.

Another way of resolving the problem would be to regard God as limited in either power or goodness, or both. Perhaps evil is due to a recalcitrant material which God is doing his best to straighten out or, perhaps, some recalcitrant streak in God's own character which he is still trying to tame. The former option was urged by the school of Boston Personalism, while both have been asserted by various process theologians. Such "finite theisms" are certainly worthy of consideration, but it is clear that any such position represents a major modification of traditional theism which once more seems to conflict with essential elements of the great theistic religions. Before accepting some such view, it is wise to see whether traditional theism has within it the resources to solve the problem of evil.

The Logical Form of the Problem

One of the more well-known statements of the logical form of the problem of evil comes from the contemporary philosopher J. L. Mackie. Mackie states the problem this way: It is contradictory to affirm that God exists and is wholly good and omnipotent, and yet to admit that evil exists.[3] Mackie admits that the contradiction is not immediately obvious; to show it, he says, some additional premises must be added which spell out the meaning of terms like "good," "evil" and "omnipotent."

> These additional principles are that good is opposed to evil, in such a way that a good thing always eliminates evil as far as it can, and that there are no limits to what an omnipotent

thing can do. From these it follows that a good omnipotent thing eliminates evil completely, and then the propositions that a good omnipotent thing exists, and that evil exists, are incompatible.[4]

Mackie is claiming that the proposition "God exists," and his additional premises, logically imply that evil does not exist, which obviously contradicts the proposition that evil does exist.

Theistic responses to Mackie's argument (and other similar arguments) have centered around Mackie's claim that a good being would always eliminate evil as far as it can. There seem to be quite a few circumstances in which a good being allows evil which could be eliminated to occur, because eliminating the evil would also eliminate a good which is great enough to "outweigh" the evil which is allowed. For example, a heroic soldier might fall on a live grenade to save his comrades. His death is surely an evil, yet his action in bringing about this evil is nonetheless the action of a good person. Perhaps by diving into a trench the soldier could save his own life and prevent that evil, but to do so would result in a greater evil. So the good which is brought about by his action outweighs the evil.

So it does not seem to be true that a good being always eliminates evil as far as it can. What is true, perhaps, is that a good being always eliminates evil as far as it can without the loss of a greater good or the occurrence of a greater evil. Almost all theodicies base their arguments on this sort of "greater good" principle. The evil which God permits is justified because allowing that evil allows for the achievement of a greater good or the prevention of a greater evil.

The critic is likely to object at this point that an omnipotent being must be able to eliminate evil completely without any net loss of good or increase of evil. For, unlike our heroic soldier, an omnipotent being is supposed to be able to do anything.

The response to this has traditionally been that not even an omnipotent being can do literally anything. One limitation on omnipotence which has generally been accepted by theists, we noted in chapter two, is that not even God can do what is logically impossible. An omnipotent being cannot make a square circle, or create a person who is not a person, because these contradictory notions are not genuine possibilities. It seems plausible that the possibility or actuality of some evils is logically necessary if certain goods are to be achieved.

Various kinds of goods and evils have been claimed to be related in this way, giving rise to various types of theodicies. For example, certain kinds of moral virtues seem to logically require certain evils. Physical courage seems inconceivable without the possibility of physical pain. Perhaps some of the "first order" evils in the world, particularly the natural evils, are necessary obstacles which must exist in order for human beings to culti-vate certain "second order" virtues. This might be termed a "soul-making" theodicy.

The difficulties with a soul-making theodicy are plentiful. One problem is that not all natural evils seem to contribute to any worthwhile good—the suffering of some animals, for example. A second problem is that in addition to making possible second-order goods, such as courage, first-order evils such as pain also make possible second-order evils, such as cowardice. It is therefore not clear that allowing such evils clearly leads to a greater good.

Most theists respond to this last problem by incorporating a soul-making theodicy into another kind of theodicy, the free-will theodicy. The reason that second-order evils such as cowardice occur, as well as much other evil, is that human beings make bad use of their freedom. The resulting evil is due to human desire, not God.

But why should God give humans free will, and why should he allow them to use it so badly? Traditionally, God is said to allow freedom because without it humans could not be morally responsible agents, capable of freely doing good by responding to and loving their Creator. In creating human beings, God desired to make creatures who would freely love and serve him. The "love" of a robot who can do nothing else is not worth much. True freedom involves great risk but also the possibility of great good which can be achieved in no other way.

But why couldn't God give humans free will and guarantee that they would use their freedom wisely? The reply to this is that it simply is not logically possible for God to do this. In the sense of freedom which is required for moral responsibility, a person who is free to do action A is also free not to do A. If God guaranteed that a person in a certain situation would only do A, then that person simply would not be free with respect to A in that situation. It is logically possible for God to create free beings who always choose to do right, but it is not logically possible for God to create free beings who *inevitably* do right. If God creates beings who are truly free, then whether they do right is at least sometimes up to them and not to God.

Difficulties for such a free-will theodicy are plentiful. Obviously, such a theodicy is no more valid than the underlying theory of free will it embodies. The free-will question is a vexed one that we cannot hope to resolve here.[5] Another difficulty is that the free-will theodicy appears to account for only moral evil. To account for natural evil, the free-will argument would have to be extended in one of two ways. One way would be to see natural evil as the work of superhuman free beings, such as Satan and his angels; this thinking converts natural evil into moral evil. Another possibility would be to see natural evil as in some way a consequence of moral evil, perhaps by interpreting it as a divine judgment on a fallen race. There is biblical support for the idea that the current state of affairs in nature is an unnatural consequence of sin.[6]

Critics of theism will certainly question how one can know that natural evil should be viewed in such a way. I think it must be admitted that as full-fledged theodicies neither free-will arguments alone, nor such arguments taken in conjunction with a soul-making argument, are totally convincing. When all is said and done, it is difficult for the theist to be confident that she truly understands why God allows all the evil which does occur.

Fortunately for the theist, to rebut the logical form of the problem of evil it is not necessary to have a full-fledged theodicy. For the charge of the atheist in this case is that theism is self-contradictory. To rebut this charge it is not necessary to *know* God's actual reasons for allowing evil, or to be able to explain why God allows the evils he does. It is sufficient to know that there are *possible* reasons why an all-good, omnipotent being might allow evil, if one wishes to show that the occurrence of evil and the existence of God are not *logically* contradictory. The charge of contradiction that Mackie and others bring is a strong one, and the burden of proof is on them to show exactly what the contradiction is. No one has so far been able to do this.

As theodicies, the soul-making and free-will arguments may have their limitations, but their value in producing a *defense* against the logical form of the problem of evil may still be great. The free-will argument, for example, shows that it is not necessarily correct to say that a good being always eliminates all the evil it can, or that an omnipotent being could eliminate all evil without the loss of any greater good. Yet in order to show that theism is self-contradictory, some such premises as these must be necessarily true.

The Evidential Form of the Problem

Many atheists at this point retreat to a weaker position, but one which is nonetheless potentially damaging to the theist. They admit that theism is logically consistent and that the existence of evil does not in itself disprove the existence of God. The charge which they make is that the occurrence of evil constitutes powerful evidence against God's existence. Evil, or at least the amounts of evil and kinds of evil which occur in our world, provides us with good reasons for not believing in God.

The evidential form of the problem of evil can be best understood as a response to the "greater good" theodicies sketched in the last section. In this case the atheist admits that it is possible for a good, omnipotent being to allow evil, if by so doing a greater good is achieved. So the mere existence of evil does not contradict God's existence. However, the atheist will urge that much of the actual evil which we observe in the world is pointless; it does not appear to lead to any greater good. A good God would surely not allow that sort of evil. The argument can be summarized as follows:

1. If God exists, he does not allow any utterly pointless evil.
2. Probably, there is pointless evil.
3. Probably, God does not exist.

In responding to the evidential form of the problem, the theist can once more rely on the theodicies we examined in the last section, as well as others which have been proposed.[7] But suppose he does not find any or all of these arguments convincing? It must not be forgotten that evil is a problem felt by the believer as well as the nonbeliever. Many believers find the occurrence of many evils in the world baffling and troubling. They wonder why God allows these things, for they often do appear to be pointless. What then can the believer say?

At this point the value of the defense, as opposed to a theodicy, becomes evident. For what the believer can say at this point is that she believes God has reasons for allowing evil, even if she does not know what those reasons are. What evidence does the theist have to back up this claim? Her evidence here must simply be her evidence for God's existence and goodness. If the believer has good reasons to believe in a good God, then she also has a reason to believe that God has reasons for allowing evil. The following argument is just as *valid* as the atheistic argument just stated:

1. If God exists, he does not allow any utterly pointless evil.

2. God exists.

3. Therefore, there is no utterly pointless evil.

Which argument is to be preferred here? The answer requires that an individual make a judgment about her total evidential situation. The existence of evil *is* a problem for the theist. It does "count against" the existence of God.[8] The question at issue is whether this negative evidence is sufficient to count *decisively* against God's existence. If one has strong reasons for believing in God and for believing him good, then evil will be regarded as a difficulty, since one does not understand why God allows evil, but not as a decisive difficulty. After all, it is hard to see how finite human beings, with our imperfect and selective understanding of the ultimate meaning and pattern of the universe, could claim to know that any evil *is* utterly pointless. If through religious experience and revelation one had come to know God as a loving, good being, one would have powerful evidence that God must have reasons for allowing evil, even if we do not know what those reasons are.

It is, in fact, in just this sort of situation that faith is called for. If the faith is to be reasonable, of course, there must be some basis for belief in God. But adherents of a religion normally claim to have evidence of this type. For example, Christians usually cite the Incarnation of Jesus as providing them with knowledge of God and God's character. Jesus' death and resurrection, while not an explanation of why God allows evil, are a demonstration that he loves his creatures to the point of suffering with them and for them, and that he will eventually triumph over evil by turning it to good.

Evil then is a serious problem for the theist, but it is not necessarily an insurmountable one. If the theist has good reasons for believing in God, then he also has good reasons for believing that God is justified in permitting evil. In that case, the occurrence of evil is seen as a test of one's faith in God.

To the atheist, evil constitutes strong evidence against God's existence. From a theistic perspective, however, the person who doubts God because of the occurrence of evil needs one of two things. If he does not know God and God's goodness, he needs through experience or perhaps special revelation to come to know God or come to know God in a fuller way. If he already knows God and his goodness, then he needs pastoral encouragement that will help him persevere in his faith.

7

The Problem of Religious Language

We have examined a variety of arguments against the reasonableness of religious belief. These arguments purport to show that God can be proved not to exist or that his existence is implausible or unlikely. They represent the traditional way of supporting belief in atheism or agnosticism.

In the twentieth century a new type of challenge has arisen for religious believers. This new challenge is directed against the *meaningfulness* of belief in God. The claim is that propositions like "God exists" or "God loves human beings" are cognitively meaningless; they lack any clear sense. It's not that we lack evidence that God exists but that we do not even know what it means to say that God exists. This is the problem of religious language.

The Challenge of Logical Positivism

The charge that religious beliefs are cognitively meaningless was first made by philosophers known as logical positivists. Although logical positivism originated with a group of philosophers in Vienna, who after World War I formed the "Vienna Circle," it became known to English-speaking readers mainly through A. J. Ayer's *Language, Truth and Logic,* first published in 1936 and still in print.

The heart of logical positivism, and the basis of its attacks on the meaningfulness of religious belief, was the verifiability theory of meaning. This theory was an attempt to specify the conditions under which a proposition is meaningful. According to this theory there are two types of meaningful statements. *Analytic* propositions are those statements whose truth or falsehood is determined by the meanings of the words in the statement. According to the positivists, these would include definitions and the truths of mathematics and logic. All nonanalytic meaningful statements are *synthetic.* All synthetic propositions must be empirically verifiable by some set of sense-experiences.

On the positivist view, analytic statements do not give us any information about extralinguistic realities, since they are solely about language. To give information about reality, or "matters of fact," a proposition must be synthetic and therefore must be empirically verifiable. Since many theological statements purport to give information about God, who is supposed to be more than a linguistic reality, these statements must be empirically verifiable to be meaningful. The positivists claimed that theological assertions were not verifiable and that such statements were therefore cognitively meaningless.

According to Ayer, the positivist view rules out not only theism but also atheism and agnosticism; if "God exists" is meaningless, it can be neither affirmed nor denied nor even proposed as a possibility whose truth is not ascertainable.[1] However, in a more extended sense, positivism certainly leads to atheism, if by an atheist we mean someone who declares it is unreasonable to believe in God or even seriously to consider belief as a possibility.

Although logical positivism was popular for a period in Anglo-American philosophy, and although some of its characteristic themes continue to surface in other forms (as we shall see), it has not survived as a philosophical movement in its original form. Several powerful objections have been raised against the verifiability theory of meaning.

First, it is not clear that the verifiability theory can pass its own test as a meaningful statement. The theory certainly does not seem to be empirically verifiable, so its proponents must take it as an analytic statement, a statement about the meaning of "meaning." However, most people do not use "meaning" in the way positivists wish to, so as a dictionary definition the theory is probably false. The only option for the positivist is to propose his theory as a reform, a new stipulation as to the meaning of "meaning." But why should the theist accept this new proposal, with its devastating consequences for religious belief?

Other problems beset the verifiability theory which may be even more serious. Foremost among these is clarifying the notion of "verification." Positivism is a form of empiricism, the philosophy which wishes to ground all knowledge in experience. The positivist is suspicious of what cannot be directly seen, touched, felt and so on. As originally developed, therefore, the positivists interpreted verification to be *direct* sensory verification.

The claim that all meaningful synthetic statements must be directly verifiable led to problems, however, for many of the entities postulated by the natural sciences are not directly observable. Quarks and black holes are contemporary examples. Yet logical positivists did not wish their theory of meaning to imply that scientific assertions are meaningless. To prevent this from occurring, the theory was weakened to allow that a statement was meaningful if it could be verified indirectly. Furthermore, the positivists admitted that the verification did not have to be conclusive, since general statements such as scientific laws can never be proved to be true by any finite set of observations and that even this indirect, inconclusive verification had to be possible only in principle. When weakened in these ways, the theory conceded that religious statements (and indeed just about all statements) can be cognitively meaningful.

Various attempts were made to tighten up the principle to exclude religious statements, but these tightened versions once more were found to exclude scientific statements as well. No one, in fact, has been able to state a version of the verifiability theory liberal enough to allow meaning to science and at the same time restrictive enough to rule out religious beliefs.[2] Thus, although a few well-known philosophers such as Kai Nielsen still maintain that religious beliefs are cognitively meaningless because they are not empirically verifiable, it is hard to see why religious believers should regard such accusations with much concern.[3]

Flew's Challenge: Are Religious Beliefs Falsifiable?

In the 1950s a debate about the meaningfulness of religious language was provoked by Antony Flew. Flew borrowed a parable from another philosopher to explain why he believed religious assertions were not cognitively meaningful:

> Once upon a time two explorers came upon a clearing in the jungle. In the clearing were growing many flowers and many weeds. One explorer says, "Some gardener must tend this plot." The other disagrees, "There is no gardener." So they pitch their tents and set a watch. No gardener is ever seen. "But perhaps he is an invisible gardener." So they set up a barbed-wire fence. They electrify it. They patrol with blood-hounds. . . . But no shrieks ever suggest that some intruder has received a shock. No movements of the wire ever betray an invisible climber. The bloodhounds never give cry. Yet still the Believer is not convinced. "But there is a gardener,

invisible, intangible, insensible to electric shocks, a gardener who has no scent and makes no sound, a gardener who comes secretly to look after the garden which he loves." At last the Skeptic despairs, "But what remains of your original assertion? Just how does what you call an invisible, intangible, eternally elusive gardener differ from an imaginary gardener or even from no gardener at all?"[4]

Flew goes on to claim that "sophisticated religious believers" are similar to the believer in the parable in that they do not admit that any conceivable event or series of events would provide us with a sufficient reason for admitting that propositions like "God loves us" or "God exists" are false. Religious believers assert that God loves us, yet all kinds of horrible disasters are allowed by God to occur, events which a loving God presumably could and would prevent. Such events do not falsify the claim that "God loves us." Instead the believer qualifies or weakens the claim by adding that God's love is inscrutable or mysterious. At this point Flew wonders whether the original assertion is still meaningful or whether, like the claim of the believer in the parable, it has "died the death of a thousand qualifications." In other words, Flew challenges the believer to specify what would count as a falsification of his religious claims; and he argues that if nothing could falsify those claims, then the claims are vacuous.

Flew's challenge appears to differ from the logical positivist view in two ways. First, Flew speaks of falsification rather than verification. Second, he roots his challenge not in a dubious general theory of language, such as the verifiability theory, but in the basic insight that to assert something is to deny something else. An assertion which does not rule out anything, but rather is compatible with any conceivable state of affairs, does not appear to assert anything either.

The differences may be more apparent than substantive, however. Suppose the believer responded to Flew's challenge by saying that theological assertions are certainly *not* compatible with just anything. "God exists," for example, would be falsified by God's not existing. If God hated us that would falsify "God loves us." Flew would almost certainly not accept this as a response to his challenge, because he would probably regard these assertions as equally "metaphysical" and meaningless. What Flew really wants is some set of empirically observable conditions which would falsify theological assertions. If this is correct, then Flew's challenge seems to presuppose something like a verificationist theory of meaning, at least in one of its weaker versions. If so, and this verificationist theory is suspect, it does not seem that it would be a fatal blow if religious beliefs fail to meet Flew's challenge.

Responses to Flew

Though it is not obvious that religious beliefs must be empirically falsifiable in Flew's sense, it would be damaging if religious beliefs turned out to have no empirical consequences, or if experience were simply irrelevant to such beliefs. For this reason it is worthwhile to examine a number of attempts to meet Flew's challenge.

Hare's blik *proposal and noncognitive theories of religious language.* One of the first respondents to Flew was R. M. Hare, who conceded that Flew was basically right about the falsifiability of religious beliefs but wrong about the implications of this. As Hare saw it, religious beliefs are not really cognitive assertions because they are not falsifiable. Nevertheless, they are meaningful and important.

Hare interprets religious beliefs as *bliks*, a term he coined. Hare explains a blik by his own parable:

A certain lunatic is convinced that all dons want to murder him. His friends introduce him to all the mildest and most respectable dons that they can find, and after each of them has retired, they say, "You see, he doesn't really want to murder you, he spoke to you in a most cordial manner; surely you are convinced now?" But the lunatic replies, "Yes, but that was only his diabolical cunning; he's really plotting against me the whole time, like the rest of them."[5]

As Hare sees it, bliks are like unfalsifiable convictions; they are not assertions, therefore, but it is nevertheless important to have the "right" blik, presumably because of the impact bliks have on our conduct.

The concept of a blik is introduced through the example of a lunatic, but sane people also have bliks. For example, all normal people are convinced that our past experience is a good guide to the future. Religious beliefs are a different kind of blik—not insane, but not universally shared either.

While a provocative notion, Hare's concept of bliks ultimately does not seem coherent to me. Hare says that bliks are not assertions, but he also talks about bliks' being right or wrong. He fails to explain how nonassertions can be right or wrong.

I suspect Hare's proposal is an inconsistent mix of two different responses to Flew. His notion of a blik bears some resemblance to the concept of an "ultimate presupposition," developed by R. G. Collingwood and others. An ultimate presupposition is a fundamental metaphysical conviction which is used as a basis for interpreting all of one's experiences. Such presuppositions are not falsifiable precisely because they are ultimate. Such presuppositions are cognitive, however. To go this route, Hare would have to reject the verificationist thesis that an unfalsifiable statement is always cognitively meaningless.

The other response which Hare was perhaps developing with his notion of bliks is the noncognitive view of religious assertions. Empiricist philosophers such as R. B. Braithwaite have accepted Flew's conclusion that religious statements are not cognitive assertions, but have then gone on to argue that they may be noncognitively meaningful because of their practical value.[6] To put it simply, a proposition such as "God is love," rather than asserting a transcendent metaphysical reality, may be a disguised imperative or a piece of moral guidance. Perhaps it is equivalent to something like "A person ought to regard love as the most important thing in life." This noncognitive theory rejects as improper questions about whether religious statements are factually true: religion is here reduced to a "way of life," with the traditional beliefs which were a part of that way of life transformed into "myths," "symbols" or "illustrative parables." As Braithwaite sees it, it is the use of such parables and stories in religions which differentiates religion from mere morality. The illustrative elements are important, therefore, but it is not important whether or not the stories are true.

Another example of a noncognitive theory might be theologian Paul Tillich's "symbol" theory.[7] For Tillich, God must not be thought of as a being, but rather as "being-itself" or "the power of being." Different religious communities employ different "symbols" which have the power to evoke or disclose the meaning or power of "being-itself." These "symbols" for Tillich do not represent facts; hence they cannot be falsified by any empirical evidence. Their "truth" or "falsity" consists of their ability to evoke or disclose the "power of being" to the religious community.

Someone who has given up on traditional religious beliefs could certainly adopt such a noncognitive view of religion if he believed it worthwhile to attempt to save religion as a cultural institution. But the religion which would be saved would certainly have undergone a profound transformation. It is true that religious beliefs have profound, far-reaching implications for one's way of life. But it is questionable whether these practical implications can be divorced from the beliefs which formed their traditional basis. Religious believers do claim that "love should be the most important thing in life," but they claim this is true *because* God exists, whose nature is love, and because human beings were created in God's image.

Mitchell: religious beliefs as falsifiable in principle but not in practice. Basil Mitchell's response to Flew seems much closer to the way religious people typically regard their faith than does Hare's blik proposal. Essentially, Mitchell argues that religious beliefs are assertions and that they are falsifiable in principle. Believers are not, however, able to say precisely what would count as a falsification, which implies that in practice we may not be able to say with certainty whether such beliefs have been falsified.

Mitchell explains his view with a parable as well.[8] In an occupied country during a war, a resistance fighter meets a mysterious stranger and spends a night in earnest conversation. The stranger tells the fighter that he is on the side of the resistance, even in command of it, and he begs him to have faith in him no matter what happens. The stranger is hereafter seen only from a distance, sometimes doing things which obviously help the resistance, sometimes doing things which appear to betray it. How long should the resistance fighter maintain his faith in the stranger? Mitchell does not think it possible to say precisely when such faith becomes unreasonable.

It is not that the apparently unfriendly acts of the stranger do not count as evidence against his faithfulness. The question is whether those acts should be allowed to count *decisively* against the favorable evidence, buttressed as it is by one's faith in the stranger. The resistance fighter has a choice between concluding that the stranger is not really on his side, or concluding that he is on his side but has reasons for sometimes behaving strangely. Both assertions are clearly meaningful, but it is not always clear when the evidence is sufficient to rule one alternative out.

In a similar way, Mitchell argues, some things count against God's existence or his loving us—unexplained evil and suffering, for example. For the believer, however, these things do not count decisively, for he believes that he has sufficient evidence for God's reality and goodness. Believing that God is good, he concludes that God has reasons for his actions even if we do not know what those reasons are. Thus for Mitchell religious beliefs in principle are open to empirical disconfirmation and are thus meaningful, even if we cannot say precisely how much contrary evidence would suffice to disconfirm them.

Hick: eschatological verification. In response to Flew's challenge, John Hick has asserted that religious beliefs are not only falsifiable or verifiable in principle, as Mitchell says, but that they are conclusively so, if one takes account of the possibility of experience after death.[9] Drawing on the fact that "a survival prediction . . . is contained in the *corpus* of Christian belief," Hick has argued that experiences after death "of the fulfillment of God's purposes for ourselves, as this has been disclosed in the Christian revelation" as well as "an experience of communion with God as he has revealed himself in the person of Christ" would constitute a verification of the truth-claims, not of religion in general obviously, but of the Christian faith.[10] If true, therefore, Christian beliefs are verifiable; but if there is no afterlife, of course, there would be no experiences which would falsify the belief.

Other possible responses: historical verification. Hick's response is not only interesting in itself, but it suggests other possible responses to Flew. Hick is clearly right in seeing the truth-claims of actual religions as embedded in more comprehensive contexts. The connection between various religious beliefs may then allow some beliefs to be tested indirectly.

For example, a key element in orthodox Christian belief is the doctrine of the Second Coming of Jesus. A historical return of Jesus to earth as depicted by Paul in 1 Thessalonians 4 would appear then to be a possible eschatological test for Christianity.

The Christian faith is, moreover, bound up with doctrines about the past as well as the future. When Christians say that "God" exists, they mean to refer to "the Person who called Abram out of Ur" and "the One who raised Jesus from the dead." This raises the possibility of at least indirect historical verification (and falsification), as well as eschatological verification. Orthodox Christians, who regard Jesus' death and resurrection as genuine historical events, would appear to have beliefs which are in principle open to empirical confirmation and disconfirmation.

The kinds of religious experiences discussed in chapter four might also provide a way of confirming or disconfirming religious beliefs, and to this sort of evidence one might also add the religious dimensions of experience which provide the basis for the traditional theistic arguments.

Wittgensteinian Approaches: Religion and "Forms of Life"

It is one thing to rebut the arguments of Flew and others and to argue that religious statements are meaningful. It is quite another thing to actually analyze such statements and discern just *how* they are meaningful. The remainder of this chapter will be devoted to this more positive task. Some promising suggestions as to how this should be done can be found in the later writings of philosopher Ludwig Wittgenstein.

In his early work Wittgenstein thought of language as primarily serving the function of "stating facts," and he identified "meaning" with "factual meaning," much as did the positivists. In his later work Wittgenstein recognizes that this view of language was unduly narrow:

But how many kinds of sentences are there? . . . There are *countless* kinds: countless different kinds of use of what we call "symbols," "words," "sentences." And this multiplicity is not something fixed, given once for all; but new types of language, new language games, as we may say, come into existence, and others become obsolete and get forgotten.[11]

Wittgenstein uses the term "language-game" to emphasize "the fact that the *speaking* of language is part of an activity, or of a form of life."[12] Language is used in countless ways, and there are as many kinds of meaning as there are kinds of uses of language. Wittgenstein, in fact, enjoined his followers, "Don't look for the meaning, look for the use."

This concept of "language-games" and the correlative concept of "forms of life" are significant themes in Wittgenstein's view of language. Although Wittgenstein never developed these concepts in a precise manner, they have been fertile and suggestive. To really understand the use of a word, says Wittgenstein, one must understand it in its context. Various "games" are played with language; the language-game of mathematics differs greatly from that of baseball. Each has its own characteristic vocabulary and "rules," which are usually not explicitly learned but are embedded in the shared practices of the respective linguistic community.

The last point highlights the connection between language-games and forms of life. To understand the use of a word, we must understand it not only in its linguistic context but in its larger, "real life" pragmatic context. We must not only understand how to use a term grammatically but also in what situations and for what purposes a language-game is played. Thus, for Wittgenstein, to imagine a language is ultimately to imagine a form of life.

It is not surprising that these Wittgensteinian themes should have been applied to religious language, which certainly seems to be a distinctive language-game which is embedded in an equally distinctive form of life. It is now generally conceded that the analysis of religious language must at least begin from an insider's perspective, one which takes into account the actual uses to which the language is put in the context of the religious community.

Some of Wittgenstein's followers, such as D. Z. Phillips, however, have developed these insights in a questionable manner. Kai Nielsen calls their work Wittgensteinian Fideism.[13] By emphasizing the distinctives of the religious language-game,

Wittgensteinian Fideism converts religious language into an autonomous sphere, with its own unique criteria of meaning and truth. If one asks whether God exists, the answer is that God is certainly real, since the term "God" is used by the religious community as a name for a reality. If one asks, "But is God *really* real?" the question betrays a misunderstanding, an assumption that there is some general concept of "reality" which can be abstracted from the particular language-game which gives the term its meaning.

What seems questionable about this is the apparent assumption that religious language and the religious form of life can be insulated and separated from other linguistic practices and life activities. When the religious believer says that God created the heavens and the earth, that God raised Jesus from the dead or that God answered his prayers for healing, he implies there are connections between religious language and the language we use to describe nature, history and the daily events of our lives. Religious language does not seem to be the "autonomous preserve" it must be for Wittgensteinian Fideism to be correct.

Sometimes the Wittgensteinians seem to come perilously close to the noncognitive view of religious language. Phillips, for example, gives an interesting analysis of "eternal life."[14] Beginning with the noncontroversial point that eternal life must not be conceived as a mere quantitative extension of this life, Phillips goes on to the controversial claim that the Christian concept of eternal life has nothing to do with factual questions about life beyond the grave, either in a disembodied form or in an actual resurrected body. Eternal life is rather a new quality of life which can be achieved now. The biblical accounts of heaven and life after death are "pictures" which must not be taken literally; they must be understood with reference to the use the pictures have in encouraging believers to strive after the type of life and attitude which is completely identified with God's purposes and which therefore can truly be said to be "eternal."

This seems perilously close to Braithwaite's analysis of religious language, or to one interpretation of Hare's bliks.

Such a reading of "eternal life" ultimately does not seem to me to be consistent with Wittgenstein's own emphases. If one looks at the actual use of "eternal life" in the religious community, one does not find any divorce between the belief that it is possible for individuals to experience communion with God now and after death and the encouraging uses which this belief serves. It is quite true that the ordinary Christian sees eternal life as something which can be possessed now, at least partially, and quite true that life after death is not a mere quantitative extension of this life. However, the ordinary believer certainly regards eternal life, with its qualitative character, as in some way a fact which will be verified in experiences beyond the grave. It is hardly a "mere picture" whose meaning is exhausted by its this-worldly use.

The Thomistic Doctrine of Analogy

Philosophers in the twentieth century are not the first to grapple with the question of religious language. In the thirteenth century Thomas Aquinas developed a sophisticated and influential theory. According to Aquinas, when we speak about God we inevitably must use language originally developed for finite creatures. Such language cannot be used to apply to God precisely in its original sense.

When we speak about God, we do not speak univocally, which is to use the same term in precisely the same sense; nor do we speak equivocally, which is to use the same term in two unrelated senses, as when one uses the term *race* to refer to an athletic contest on one occasion and an ethnically related group of human beings on another. Rather, talk about God is analogical, which is to use the same term in a similar or related sense.[15] One might, for example, call both a dog and a person faithful. In this case there is a resemblance between a faithful person and a faithful dog; the term is not being used equivocally. Nevertheless, faithfulness in a person is not identical with faithfulness in a dog.

Aquinas defines two major types of analogy. The *analogy of attribution* uses a term originally employed for one thing for a second thing because of a causal relation between the two things. Thus, one calls a certain geographical location "healthy" because it causes the people who live there to be healthy, and one calls a rosy complexion "healthy" because it is the effect of a healthy body. Religious people use terms like "living" and "loving" to refer to God because he is the cause of life and love in his creation.

The other type of analogy is the *analogy of proportionality*. Here a term is employed to refer to something proportionately to the kind of reality the thing possesses. A dog is brave in the way dogs can be brave, in proportion to its reality as a dog. A human being's bravery is proportionately richer because her nature is richer. God is loving, holy and powerful, but he possesses all these qualities in proportion to his infinite nature; human love, holiness and power resemble but fall far short of these qualities in God.

The analogy theory is often criticized on the grounds that one must be able to reformulate an analogy in literal, univocal language for the analogy to be meaningful. Unless we know precisely how God's love resembles human love, so the argument goes, we do not really know what it means to say God is loving. But to know how God's love resembles human love, we must know what that love is like and be able to describe it univocally.[16]

Whether this objection is sound is controversial. But it seems to me that all this objection really establishes, if one is inclined to accept it, is that it must be possible *in principle* to replace analogous language with univocal language, not that this replacement must be actually carried out for analogous language to have meaning. If an analogy is valid, then a person who has sufficient knowledge and has a language sufficiently rich should be able to describe the analogous relationship in a direct fashion. However, it is surely too strong to claim that analogous language is meaningless unless it can be "cashed in" with univocal language. If that were the case, what need would we have for analogous language? Analogies would be proper in that case only where they were unnecessary. Surely the uses of analogy, metaphor and other nonunivocal discourse in poetry, and even scientific model-building,[17] show that such language is useful and meaningful, even where we are not yet able to dispense with such language, and perhaps even if we are not able to do this at all.

The objection may also presuppose an overly wooden view of "literal" language, and an overly sharp dichotomy between such language and the language of analogy. Many ordinary, literal terms began their careers as metaphors. It is hard to see how language could creatively develop and new concepts be originated if a nonliteral usage were always meaningless until it could be replaced by a more literal statement.

It is true that Aquinas's analogy theory implies that we lack a clear and precise understanding of God and his characteristics. We only know God as the being who resembles though surpasses what we humans know as "love," "power," "holiness" and so on. However, it is quite in keeping with ordinary religious belief to claim that God is in some ways essentially mysterious. Our knowledge of God is not supposed to be theoretically and scientifically precise; it has an essentially practical purpose. It may be sufficient for human beings if they have enough of an understanding of God to know how to relate to him properly. If it turns out that humans, in this life at least, lack any knowledge of God's essence, as Aquinas claims, this will not faze the believer, so long as she has enough of an idea of God to know how to worship and serve him properly.

The Multiple Functions of Religious Language

No theory of religious language has yet emerged that has won general acceptance, and perhaps none ever will. However, it should now be clear that religious language is an extremely complicated phenomenon, serving many purposes and functioning in many different contexts. It seems plausible that any adequate theory will have to be a complex one which recognizes this variety.

The Wittgensteinians are probably on the right track in urging us to consider first the uses of religious language. As Wittgenstein himself notes, we learn what it means to say "God's eye is upon us" by learning what inferences believers draw and do not draw from such a statement. From this statement it would be proper to infer that God is aware of what I am doing when I lie and no human finds me out; it would be improper to infer that God has eyebrows. Theological statements form an interconnected web, and the meaning of any one statement is contextually shaped.

Even more important, as the Wittgensteinians stress, is the "real-life use" of religious talk. Someone who could only talk about God's creating the world, but who had no understanding that this implied that a person ought to worship God and have an appropriate humility in recognizing that her talents are *gifts,* would certainly not have a genuinely religious understanding of such a belief. It is an essential feature of most religious claims that they have implications for how one should live. This practical dimension of religion, while not the whole story as some noncognitive approaches suggest, is an absolutely crucial feature of religious language.

An adequate theory of religious language must also come to terms with the cognitive dimension. This dimension comes to the fore partly in the interpretive and explanatory power of theological systems. This can be seen in the theistic arguments when taken individually but even more when regarded collectively. The explanatory function of religious language may, in fact, provide us with ways of speaking literally and univocally about God. Yet religious beliefs do not merely provide us with a theoretical web which helps to make sense of experience as a whole. They also make contact with experience in a piecemeal way. This can be seen in the responses to Flew's challenge. At least in the case of Christianity, theology makes contact with evidence through specific facts of history, through the believer's ongoing religious experiences, and in some fairly definite eschatological predictions about the future.

For orthodox Christians, in all these aspects the believer's understanding of religious language is heavily shaped by what is taken to be an authoritative revelation. The Christian believer does not merely have an understanding of God in the abstract, but God as revealed in the person of Jesus. Though it is probably correct to maintain that a person must have *some* awareness of God already to understand what it means to say Jesus is the Son of God, it is certainly the case that historical events and parables can vastly enrich, extend and even overturn, to some extent, the believer's understanding of God. The believer does not understand God merely as Creator but as the Father of the Jesus whom he has accepted as Lord. Jesus' own life, as well as the parables he told, becomes, in Ian Crombie's term, an *authorized parable,* a picture of God which is accepted as trustworthy because of the trust one has placed in Jesus.[18]

8

Religious Pluralism and Personal Faith

Our contemporary religious situation differs markedly from that faced by people a few hundred years ago. In Europe prior to the Reformation, the idea that one was faced with a plurality of religious beliefs, from which one had to choose, was foreign to the great majority of people. Religious beliefs were passed down from generation to generation. Certainly individuals may have had questions and doubts, and certainly people were faced with choices as to how to interpret and apply what was passed down to them, but those doubts and choices still presupposed a certain framework which could be taken for granted.

In today's world few people enjoy such a situation. Daily contacts through education and, perhaps most powerfully, through mass media bring home to us the existence of radically different religious options. For example, Christians face not only the in-house disagreements with other Christians which have proliferated since the Reformation, but many other world religions, as well as the secular mentality which opts for no overt religious belief at all. In such a situation, hardly anyone is content to believe what they believe simply because it was passed on to them by their parents or local church. People are troubled by whether their faith is a mere provincial bias or historical accident; they want to know whether they have grounds for thinking their belief to be genuinely true.

Philosophy of religion, as a no-holds-barred critical dialog, is thus a crucial endeavor in today's world. But it is not without risk, since the outcome of such a dialog may be merely increased doubt and confusion. This book itself could serve as an illustration of the continuing debate among philosophers about the reasonableness of belief in God, the problem of evil, the possibility of miracles, the proper analysis of religious experience and many other such topics. A crucial cluster of questions emerges as we deal with religious commitment in a pluralistic world. In a world such as ours, *can* a person commit himself or herself decisively to a particular set of religious beliefs? *Should* a person do so? Are such commitments reasonable?

The first question is largely a psychological and sociological one, and the answer seems to be yes, at least for many people. Though a larger number of agnostics may exist now than in previous eras, great numbers of people still adhere firmly to religious positions. And there continue to be instances of conversion where people who once had no faith come to believe, or acquire a new faith. One must include in the group of "committed people" those who are committed atheists as well as religious believers. The label "secular man" can cover many types of individuals, from the person who scarcely gives religion a thought to the "evangelistic atheist" who is committed to getting people to abandon their "superstitions" and embrace an atheistic creed.

The question of most interest to the philosopher, however, is not whether it is psychologically possible to be religiously committed, positively or negatively, but whether such commitments are reasonable. In the remainder of this chapter we shall pursue this question, first in general terms and then with reference to the plurality of world religions with their competing truth-claims.

Faith: Subjectivity in Religious Arguments

The student who enters the critical dialog we have called philosophy of religion may initially hope that rational reflection will eliminate the pluralism of competing perspectives. But such a hope seems doomed to disappointment. It appears rather that the disagreements which are present among people in general reappear among philosophers.

Why does such disagreement continue to exist? There are doubtless many reasons. One important one, which we shall explore later, is that religious beliefs impinge directly on the way a person should live. To accept or reject a religion is to accept or reject a whole way of life, and such decisions always involve the emotions as much as the intellect. It is not surprising that people who do not want to live as Christians, and who want Christianity to be false, should find reasons to justify their beliefs.

A second reason for disagreement among philosophers of religion has to do with the subjective commitments, the "gut convictions," which philosophers as human beings bring to their analyses of the arguments. In our examination of the arguments for and against religious belief we stumbled on this factor again and again. Ultimately, whether an argument is judged sound depends on the truth of its premises. In many cases, a key premise is claimed to be reasonable or plausible by one individual, while another finds that premise doubtful at best.

The ontological argument, for example, seems sound if it is granted that it is reasonable to accept the claim that "God's existence is possible." The cosmological argument will be judged sound if one accepts as sound the principle of sufficient reason, especially if one interprets the experience of cosmic wonder as evidence of the contingency of the natural world. The teleological argument will be judged sound if one interprets certain phenomena in the natural world as examples of beneficial order. Is the design we see around us genuine or merely apparent? The moral argument will be judged compelling if certain views about the nature of morality are accepted.

On the other side, the argument from evil against God's existence requires one to judge whether he knows the evil in the world to be utterly pointless, or whether his grounds for believing in its pointlessness are superior to his grounds for believing in a good God. Similar comments could be made about the arguments concerning the possibility of miracles, revelation claims and the analysis of religious experience.

In looking at the "objective" arguments pro and con, it seems as if we are continually thrust back to personal, subjective judgments—to that moment where an individual simply says, "This has the ring of truth." As a result some have concluded that such rational reflection is of little value. In the end, doesn't it all boil down to a "leap of faith," a blind decision unsupported by reason?

We must begin by noting that if one wishes to speak of leaps of faith, the religious believer is not the only one who does the leaping. The basic convictions which shape the conclusions of the atheist in these matters are equally subjective.

The leap-of-faith metaphor, however, is misleading in several respects. The metaphor conjures up an image of a person who simply makes an arbitrary choice to believe or not to believe. But it does not seem possible in normal cases to simply decide to believe something. We can only believe what seems true to us, because a belief is a belief that something is *true*. No matter how hard I try, I cannot make myself believe that the Soviet Union does not exist, regardless of how comforting such a belief might be.

It is true that *faith* plays a key role in the judgments we ultimately make about religious questions. But what the leap-of-faith image misses is that the faith which is crucial is not, for the most part, faith which a person can simply manufacture by a momentary act of will. The faith which shapes the individual's judgments is rather a faith which the individual already possesses. This faith consists of the basic convictions, attitudes and values which the person *brings to* her reflection on the religious situation.

This faith, of course, is not unalterable. It can be developed and changed. Both rational reflection and moments of decision play important roles in the process of developing or altering faith. But if one is to talk of faith in connection with the judgments one makes about religious matters, it is crucial to see this faith as a set of long-term qualities of whole persons, not as a momentary act of the will.

Can Faith Be Reasonable?

The existence of contrasting faiths in different people accounts for a good deal of the disagreements in religion. That faith plays such a crucial role in religious judgments troubles many people. Even if faith is not seen as an arbitrary blind leap, it still seems to undermine the claims of religious believers to *know* religious truths.

Lurking behind this anxiety is the strong foundationalist epistemology which we described as neutralism in chapter one. If my judgment that a set of religious beliefs is true is partly grounded in faith convictions which are not shared by everyone, then it seems to many that such a judgment cannot be objectively certain. Is commitment reasonable in such a case? Can such a belief really amount to knowledge?

These questions raise fundamental epistemological issues

about the nature of knowledge and justification. A full treatment of them would require a fully worked-out epistemology.[1] Here we can do no more than sketch the perspective on them which seems most reasonable.

The foundationalist ideal in epistemology is "objective certainty": it seems to the foundationalist that our knowledge must be based on a foundation which is so certain as to be acceptable to any sane, reasonable person. A reasonable person is therefore one who avoids commitment in cases where the commitment cannot be objectively guaranteed. Reason and faith are therefore seen as mutually hostile. Someone who relies on personal faith commitments is being unreasonable because reason demands that an individual put aside all prejudices, preconceptions and presuppositions.

The foundationalist ideal takes many forms. In its *empiricist* form it demands that we rely solely on "objective facts" in determining our beliefs. In its *rationalist* form it asks that we begin with basic premises which are self-evident to reason. In all its forms foundationalism is an attempt to eliminate subjectivity—and risk—from the knowing process. To use John Dewey's phrase, it is "a quest for certainty"; it wants, however, not merely certainty, but an *objective* certainty in which the individual makes no risky commitments as an individual.

If foundationalism is a valid epistemological ideal, then I think one would have to admit that religious knowledge in the foundationalist sense of the term, whether positive or negative, is not really possible. The subjective element in such judgments seems ineradicable, at least in this life. But is foundationalism a valid ideal?

Philosophically, foundationalism has come under strong attack. Almost no one would today defend it in the strong version sketched above, though there may be some weaker versions which are still tenable. Rationalists have been thrown on hard times by the difficulty of finding enough self-evident truths to be a basis for knowledge. Empiricists have been embarrassed by the increasing recognition that the "hard facts" of experience are not always so hard. What one observes is strongly shaped by prior expectations, and experience seems to be heavily influenced by the conceptual framework of the experiencer. A further problem for the empiricist concerns getting from the "facts" to general theories which seem to be "underdetermined" by those facts.[2]

Perhaps a more straightforward way of deciding the viability of foundationalism is to see whether it is an ideal which we regard as valid in fields other than religion. Once more, foundationalism seems to be in trouble. In everyday life, individuals make countless judgments which they regard as reasonable but which cannot be justified on foundationalist grounds.

I meet a new individual at school. After a few minutes' conversation I form an opinion of the person as a likable, trustworthy man, and I invite him to my home to pursue a possible friendship. As the friendship grows, my confidence in the character of my friend becomes stronger and stronger. If I could articulate the grounds for such a judgment, which may not even be possible, I should discover that these grounds rest heavily on the faith assumptions which I brought to the relationship. At each stage of the relationship I make interpretive judgments which are hardly infallible and which someone who approached the relationship with a different set of expectations and attitudes might not take. Nevertheless I am confident of my judgments. I do not claim they are infallible; it is logically conceivable that my new friend is a con artist who will eventually be my undoing. But I am confident this will not be the case, for I believe in my friend.

This example is a particularly apt one for religious knowledge, since interpersonal knowledge among humans shares many features of religious knowledge. But the example is not unique.

The overwhelming majority of our everyday beliefs rest on interpretive judgments which incorporate a personal element.

Nor is such faith present only in everyday life. As was briefly noted in chapter one, philosophers of science such as Thomas Kuhn and Stephen Toulmin have argued that faith commitments play a positive role even in the sciences.[3] In becoming a scientist, an individual becomes a part of a scientific community, which is defined by the shared values, attitudes and basic assumptions of its members. These shared commitments are embodied not only in theories but in the life and practice of the community, and they are acquired not only through overt instruction but by the individual's coming to share in that communal form of life.

The foundationalist ideal does not seem then to be either realistic or desirable in areas of life other than religion. There seems little reason therefore to impose it on religion, where, it would seem, faith surely has a legitimate role to play in human life, if it has such a role anywhere. With the abandonment of the foundationalist ideal, the way seems open for developing a view of reason which will make it possible to see faith and reason as potential allies instead of competitors.

Interpretive Judgments and the Nature of a "Cumulative Case"

Foundationalism appears attractive to many because they fear that its denial will open the floodgates to superstition and nonsense. The choice which they see is one between objective certainty and a blind leap of faith, the latter meaning that "anything goes."

One way of looking at the foundationalist ideal is as a quest for an "algorithm" to decide religious questions. An algorithm is a decision procedure in mathematics which, when followed correctly, is guaranteed to lead to a solution of a problem. A finite number of steps which can be followed by anyone is the ideal. I question whether a "religious algorithm" would even be desirable. What must be attacked head-on, however, is the false disjunction of *either* an algorithm *or* an irrational leap. There is a great deal of room between these two extremes, and reasonable judgments can be made in a great many areas of human life even though algorithmic decision procedures are lacking. A key element in such areas is the concept of an *interpretive judgment*.

In his excellent book *The Justification of Religious Belief,* Basil Mitchell gives several examples of reason at work in nonalgorithmic areas.[4] One is the area of historical scholarship. Historians often disagree about the causes of a particular event, or its meaning. Though rival historians may agree on many facts, they often disagree about how these facts should be interpreted and their significance evaluated.

Another excellent example is the field of literary criticism. Literary scholars often disagree about the meaning of a poem. Is a particular line to be regarded as irony, satire or straightforward praise?

In both of these areas "objective" factors play an important role. Rival historians search for facts that will support their own theories, and they interpret the facts in accordance with their overall theory. Rival critics look for features of the poem which support their interpretation, as well as other sorts of data, such as known facts about the author's attitudes. Such disagreements may not in the end be objectively resolvable to the satisfaction of all parties. However, this does not mean that reason has no role to play in such matters. We can still distinguish between interpretations which are reasonable and those which are preposterous. In recognizing the role of interpretation and the lack of an algorithm, the floodgates to nonsense have not been thrown open.

These examples are instructive for the philosophy of religion, for *interpretation* will play a key role in defending or attacking religious beliefs as well. The proponent of the cosmological argument interprets the experience of cosmic wonder differently than her opponent. The proponent of the moral argument interprets morality differently than does his opponent. The religious individual who perceives God *through* a sermon, song or revelatory book interprets her experience very differently than does the nonreligious person.

Indeed, it is very likely that the experiences themselves differ. For in speaking of interpretation, I do not mean to refer only or even mainly to a consciously articulated process which follows experience, but also to those interpretive features which are already present in experience. We do not usually simply see or hear; we see something *as* something and hear something *as* something.

One feature of interpretation which calls for special attention is the way interpretive judgments presuppose one another. This feature is often referred to as "the hermeneutical circle," for it seems that interpretive or hermeneutical arguments are circular. One's reading of the individual parts of a text, for example, is strongly influenced by one's overall view of the text's main thrust. Yet how does one acquire an understanding of that whole apart from an understanding of the parts?

This circle, of course, is resolved by all of us when we read a book or poem. How do we do it? Initially we simply plunge in and start reading, relying on what might be termed our "pre-understanding." Drawing on any background knowledge we may have and our overall experience and judgment, we begin where we are, and we form an overall impression of what the piece is all about, one that provides us with a perspective from which to interpret as we read further. This initial hypothesis is not, however, carved in stone. It is modified and reshaped as it is put to the test of making sense of the individual texts. This "testing process" becomes even more in evidence as the individual encounters and considers rival readings.

When would we say that such an interpretive judgment is reasonable? Not, I submit, when it is the result of a presuppositionless, neutral standpoint, for such a "neutral" reader could not even begin to read the piece in question. Rather, *an interpretive judgment is reasonable when it can survive the process of critical testing.* A reasonable interpretation is one which accounts for the facts, suggests new insights, illuminates meaningful patterns and does so better than its rivals.

In this process, the subjective preferences which the individual brings to the process are more than an unavoidable nuisance; faith is part of what makes the whole business possible.

When tested, these subjective preferences cease to be merely subjective preferences. For the criteria used in testing them are *not* arbitrary, but are implicitly recognized as valid by all parties to the controversy. These criteria are factors such as the following: (1) *Logical consistency.* Does the system of beliefs contradict itself? (2) *Coherence.* This is more than bare logical consistency, which is simply the absence of contradiction. Coherence is a positive harmony, a fitting-together of beliefs into an organic whole. (3) *Factual adequacy.* Does the belief system account for all the facts? How well does it do so? (4) *Intellectual fertility.* Does a belief system give rise to new discoveries and insights, suggest new illuminating patterns, call one's attention to unnoticed dimensions of experience?

The case for or against a set of religious beliefs will necessarily appeal to those kinds of criteria. Because such criteria often have to be applied to a belief system as a whole, it seems to me that the justification for a set of religious beliefs is unlikely to consist of a single, linear argument, but of what Basil Mitchell has called a *cumulative case.*

Mitchell uses as an illustration for a cumulative case a hypothetical case of two explorers who stumble on a large depression in the ground.[5] One takes the hole to be the result of purposeful intelligence; the other does not. Somewhat later, they discover other similar depressions. The first person thinks he sees a pattern in the relations between the holes; to the other party they are just ordinary holes. Later still, they find in a cave some manuscripts, faint and obscure. The first explorer excitedly claims to have a document which in some way shows the design and function of the holes. To the second party the document is cryptic, and it is not clear that it has anything to do with the holes in question.

Mitchell means his story to be a parable of the argument between the religious believer and the unbeliever. The large hole corresponds to the experience of finitude and contingency which generates the cosmological argument. The smaller holes correspond to the considerations which fuel such arguments as the teleological and moral arguments, as well as the evidence from religious experience. The documents found in the cave correspond to alleged special revelations, in which God has perhaps spelled out the meaning of things in more detail. The case the believer wants to make will not be based on any one of these factors taken in isolation. Each individual piece of evidence involves an element of interpretation, and the force of the overall case depends both on its ability to account for each part and on its ability to show meaningful, coherent patterns among the parts.

Thus the theist finds it strange that there should be a contingent universe, and wonders why it exists. He finds it stranger still that the universe should show abundant examples of beneficial order, and that it should seem to contain a moral as well as a physical order. When he adds to these considerations the mass of religious experiences in which people claim to be aware of God, theism becomes at the very least a plausible hypothesis, a reasonable interpretation of experience. Confronted by a well-attested special revelation, which was accompanied by miracles and which provides insight into his own life, giving him a deep understanding of his basic failures and genuine needs, such a person might very reasonably become an adherent of a living religion.

The atheist can, of course, mount a cumulative case as well. But her case will be equally interpretive in nature. In both cases there is no reason for the individual to consign the whole matter of religious belief to the limbo of irrationalism. For such cases can be critically tested and reasonable judgments made about them. There is perhaps even less likelihood that total agreement will be reached in religion than in areas like literary criticism, for reasons we will discuss below. But a judgment which reflects the personal *faith* of the judges can still be a reasonable one, provided the individual is willing to put his convictions to the test.

Can Faith Be Certain?

Let us assume that a cumulative case, relying at certain points on interpretive judgments, can be constructed for a set of religious beliefs. Such a case would provide a rational basis for belief, if one is willing to admit the existence of a nonalgorithmic type of rationality. A skeptic might still object at this point that such a case could never really justify a genuine religious faith. One of the marks of a genuine religious commitment is that such commitments have an unconditional, decisive character. Such commitments are total commitments. But the evidence underlying religious belief would seem to fall short of absolute certainty. To the skeptic this means that a reasonable commitment to religious belief must always be tentative in nature. In support of this he could cite our own contention in the previous section that an openness to critical testing and revision in the light of new evidence is essential if a faith commitment is to be reasonable.

The skeptic's view at this point presupposes what some have called an ethics of belief. In this case the ethical principle seems to be that firmness of belief ought always to be proportionate to the quality of the evidence for the belief. Even if we admit the reasonableness of belief on the basis of evidence that is less than algorithmic, surely the degree of belief ought to reflect the degree of evidence, says the skeptic.

To respond to the skeptic's charge here, we must give a more careful analysis of the nature of religious belief, and the nature of belief generally. H. H. Price, in his classical study *Belief*, distinguishes two major types of theories of belief.[6] According to one view, which we shall call the mental-assent view, a belief is a mental act, an occurrence in which the mind considers a proposition and performs the act of "assenting" to it. According to the second theory, which we might call the behavioral-disposition theory, a belief is a tendency or disposition to act or behave in certain ways under certain conditions. Thus, if I believe that I reside in the state of Minnesota, that does not mean I am continually, consciously, considering that proposition. Rather the belief consists in hypothetical facts about my behavior like these: If I am asked what state I reside in, I will reply, "Minnesota"; if I stop at a gas station and ask for a map to help me find a nearby town, I will ask for a map of Minnesota.

Price concludes that neither view is completely adequate alone. The mental-assent view does not recognize the way in which beliefs express themselves in action, and it cannot explain the fact that I continue to believe things of which I am not at the moment consciously thinking. The behavioral-disposition view ignores the reality of mental acts of assent and has difficulty specifying in a noncircular way what acts and dispositions a belief consists in. Ultimately one must say, "A person who believes proposition P will perform those acts which a person who believes P will perform." Price concludes that a combined theory is best, a theory which recognizes the "dispositional" character of belief, but regards beliefs as consisting not merely in being disposed to perform overt actions but also to perform those mental acts of belief which Price terms "assentings."

Price's conclusion provides a good starting place for understanding religious belief as well. True religious belief cannot be reduced simply to behaving in a certain way. To believe that God is love is not *simply* to act in a loving manner. Rather the religious believer acts in a loving manner partly *because* he believes in God. He mentally assents to propositions like "God is real," "God is love," and "God wants me to love others." On the other hand, genuine religious belief clearly does not consist merely in mental acts of assent either. In the Christian religion, for example, true faith must make a difference to the believer's life. "Faith without works is dead," says the apostle James, and to merely assent to God's existence is to do no more than the devils, who also give intellectual assent to this.

It is not that the religious believer does not assent to certain propositions. It is rather that the very nature of those propositions is such that the person who merely assents to them intellectually shows thereby that in one important sense he does not believe them. Religious beliefs, even more than beliefs generally, have an essentially *prescriptive* role. Their very being, one might say, consists in their being more than intellectual beliefs. If they are genuine, they express themselves in action.

This characteristic of religious beliefs has great implications for the problem posed by the "proportionality principle" which is advocated by some as part of the ethics of belief. If religious beliefs consisted solely of mental "acts of assent," then it would make sense to say that such beliefs should be proportionate to the evidence, and that therefore such beliefs could not possess an "unconditional" character unless the evidence is absolutely unconditional. If religious beliefs consist mainly of dispositions to perform certain actions, however, with even the propositions to which one mentally assents having prescriptive implications for one's total life, this may not be correct. The reason for this is that many actions do not admit of degrees; they have an absolute character in the sense that one either does the action or does not.

Furthermore, many actions, if done at all, must be done in an enthusiastic, wholehearted manner. A person suffering from depression might have a choice between consulting a psychoanalyst or going to see a behavioral therapist. After reviewing the evidence as to their effectiveness, she makes a choice to see one or the other. If she actually embarks on a program of therapy, it is reasonable for her to give it her best shot and participate wholeheartedly in the program, even if she has no proof it will help her. She knows that a timid, halfhearted commitment will not give the program of therapy a fair trial. In a sense, a wholehearted commitment, far from precluding an honest test of a risky commitment, is a condition for such a test.

An even clearer illustration might be the choice to marry. A woman who is considering offers of marriage from different men has no algorithm for determining which choice is "right" for her. If she decides to marry, however, it would be the height of foolishness to refrain from committing herself wholeheartedly to the marriage on the grounds that her evidence that her husband is truly loving, kind and brave is not absolutely compelling to everyone.

Religious faith would seem to be similar. In Christianity, for example, Jesus confronts potential followers with certain claims and demands on them. Claiming to be the Son of God, he demands a willingness to sacrifice any and every finite good for him. He demanded that the rich young ruler give away all his goods and come and follow him.[7] The rich young ruler had to decide whether he really believed Jesus had the authority to make such a request and, if so, whether he wished to obey. Suppose he is willing to obey if Jesus is truly the Messiah. He reviews the evidence pro and con and decides he has good reason to believe. If he believes in Jesus, then he ought to be willing to stake everything on Jesus' words. It would not be reasonable for him to decide to give away a little of his wealth, on the grounds that he does not have absolute proof of who Jesus is. Such partial obedience would still be disobedience.

Furthermore, since most religions make predictions about the deepest experiences of believers, a wholehearted commitment may make it possible to test some of the claims of the religion in a unique way, just as a wholehearted commitment to a program of psychotherapy is an essential condition for testing the effectiveness of the program. If the rich young ruler had decided to follow Jesus, the outcome would have been significant. Would the young man by that action have gained a sense of inner peace, an understanding of what life is all about, a sense of forgiveness for his own past failures? A halfhearted, wavering faith, on the other hand, would not provide a significant test of the claims of Christianity to provide these things.

In summary, it is the nature of true religious belief that it be part of a way of life. Committing oneself to such a way of life seems to be the sort of thing which must be done in an all-or-nothing, unconditional manner, if it is to be done at all, even if the *evidence* for the commitment is a matter of degree.

This fact squares well with some other widely recognized features of religious faith. One is that religious faith is not completely or even largely a product of rational calculation. Christians, for example, insist that genuine faith is a response to what God has done for an individual, that it is not something which a person can develop simply on his own. This makes sense if faith is viewed as a total way of life and not merely as a series of mental assents. The passion which fuels such a life commitment and gives it an unconditional character is no mere intellectual belief, and it is not just the result of the reviewing of evidence. Conversely, the person who rejects religious faith also does so on grounds which are not merely rational. If religious faith makes claims on our total life, it is not surprising that many should find those claims burdensome, and that this may color the way such people view the evidence. This helps to explain the continuing lack of agreement about religious matters, among both ordinary people and critical philosophers. But to say that faith or its lack is not merely the product of rational reflection does not imply that a person cannot reflect on the reasonableness of such a commitment, nor that such reflection is unimportant.

Our argument that it may be reasonable to decisively hold a belief for which there is good but not absolutely compelling evidence does not, of course, imply that all religious beliefs must be held in this unconditional manner. Most religious believers do hold some of their beliefs in a tentative manner, recognizing them as less central to their faith than others. A Christian's belief *that* she has been redeemed by Jesus' life, death and resurrection may be more firmly held than any particular theory as to *how* this atonement was accomplished.

Faith and Doubt: Can Religious Faith Be Tested?

If one admits that a faith based on less-than-algorithmic evidence can nonetheless be "total" or decisive in character, then the opposite problem might seem to appear. Earlier we argued that a reasonable faith must be open to initial testing. But can a person who is wholeheartedly committed to a faith genuinely and honestly evaluate that faith?

It may seem that to test one's belief, one would have to be able to doubt it; and doubt seems incompatible with robust faith. But there are different kinds of doubt. Let us distinguish *logical doubt* from *existential doubt*. Logical doubt is a willingness to imaginatively consider the possibility that one's own convictions are mistaken by honestly considering the new evidence and comparing his case with other possible cumulative cases. Existential doubt is a positive belief that one's own position is seriously flawed or that it is quite possibly wrong.

A certain amount of existential doubt seems acceptable and even normal in a religious life. The great saints are not uniformly people who were never troubled by doubt, but people who were able to deal with their doubts and act decisively in spite of them.

A person willing to sacrifice her life for her faith would by no means have a faith which is somehow inferior or less than decisive, even if that person at times struggled with existential doubt. We must remember that religious beliefs are primarily dispositions to action. The test as to whether a person is truly a believer is not whether the person always mentally assents in a doubt-free manner to religious propositions. The true test is whether the person is willing to *act* on those beliefs.

Existential doubt can then coexist with religious faith. If existential doubt becomes too great or too frequent, however, faith might be crippled or cease to exist altogether. But whatever tension may be present between faith and existential doubt, there is no necessary tension between faith and logical doubt. Inherent in my belief that things are a particular way is an understanding of how things could be different. If I am genuinely convinced that my belief is true, I will not shrink from examining rival views. To the degree that I am certain and confident, I will welcome testing. A faith which evades critical questions is a faith which lacks confidence, which is *not* truly assured it has found truth. Paradoxical as it may sound, confidence in one's convictions may make it possible to put those convictions to serious test. A recognition of the logical possibility that one could be mistaken is not a reason to believe that one actually is mistaken. Similarly, an imaginative ability to empathize with a rival position so as to compare it with one's own does not mean that one is actually doubting one's beliefs existentially.

This is not to say that religious believers will or should continually seek out objections to their faith. Belief is, after all, to be lived. If we spent all our time critically reflecting on our faith, we would have no time to live out that faith. And religious faith is tested in part by the very process of living it out. Nevertheless, it is appropriate for religious believers, as they have the intellectual ability and opportunity, to spend some time reflecting on their faith and its reasonableness.

What Is Faith?

In the preceding discussion the term "faith" has been used in a variety of senses. We have used the term to refer to the assumptions, convictions and attitudes which the believer *brings to* the evidence for and against religious truth. We have also used the term to refer to the commitment which is in some respects the *outcome* of this reflection. We have used "faith" to refer to the subjective preferences of people generally and to refer to the specific kind of commitment which is involved in being a Christian. What then is faith?

Faith is all of these, though this must not be taken as implying there are no significant differences between the various kinds of faith. In a sense, every person has "faith"; everyone has deep-rooted assumptions, convictions and attitudes which color what counts as evidence for him and how that evidence is interpreted. This is the kind of faith which one brings to the evidence. Insofar as beliefs are reflected in action, and people must make choices, everyone also has faith in the sense of commitments which may or may not be informed by rational reflection.

In the ongoing life of an actual person these are simply two different moments in what might be called the faith dimension of life. The faith which we *bring to* our reflection embodies previous commitments, and the commitment which is the *outcome* of reflection is the faith which we bring to our future reflection. Faith can legitimately be thought of as both prior conviction and commitment. This movement from prior conviction through rational reflection to commitment cannot be understood merely as a temporally distinct process either. For the having of convictions, the reflecting and the committing interpenetrate each other in the most complex fashion.

This general structure of faith as the personal commitment which both informs and is in turn shaped by reflection is common to both the religious believer and nonbeliever. Both have faith in both of these senses. This does not, however, imply that religious faith has nothing distinctive about it. The content itself makes a tremendous difference. The particular kinds of attitudes, convictions and commitments which permeate the life of a genuine Christian differ radically from the attitudes, convictions and commitments which permeate the life of a consistent, clear-headed unbeliever.

Furthermore, this content may correspond to equally momentous differences in the way the person relates to that content. As we noted above, religious beliefs have an essentially prescriptive role; they are not truly believed if the belief is merely intellectual and makes no difference in the believer's life. Furthermore, again as noted above, the special character of religious belief demands an equally strong commitment on the part of the individual. The religious believer cannot regard her faith merely as a hypothesis to which she has a certain degree of commitment. The commitment must be decisive and total. The believer claims that this commitment is not a "mere opinion"; it is a conviction which she feels certain is true, a certainty which both stems from and underlies the existential commitment she has made.

It is true in one sense that "everyone has faith." But there is a special kind of faith which is uniquely religious. Even here, however, there is a plurality. Different religions engender different types of religious faith. There is therefore a distinctly Christian kind of faith, though the task of describing that faith in its details falls outside the general project of the philosophy of religion. The existence of this pluralism raises once more the question of commitment: How does one choose?

Could One Religion Be True?

The pluralism that faces the contemporary believer is most dramatically evident in the existence of competing religions. Even if we leave out Marxism and secular humanism, we still have Christianity, Judaism, Islam, Hinduism and Buddhism as active faiths with millions of adherents. Is it reasonable to commit oneself to just one of these religions? Could one religion contain the final truth?

An increasing number of people feel the answer is no for at least two reasons. First, there is the problem of tolerance and arrogance. Is it not intolerant of other faiths to claim that their own religion contains the final truth? And is not such a claim arrogant? Missionary activity and proselytizing should be replaced by dialog and mutual respect, say many religious thinkers. Second, the view that one religion contains the final truth seems provincial. Surely God has not limited his revelation to one geographical section or ethnic group.

Those who regard all religions as at least possibly true employ two different strategies. We will examine each in turn. The first option is exemplified in the work of Wilfred Cantwell Smith of Harvard University. Smith says that we should stop thinking about religious truth in propositional terms and recognize that religiously speaking it is personal lives that are true or false.[8] Smith tells of a follower of Islam he met in the Himalayas.[9] The man was selling fruit and had a primitive scale. There was no way of verifying the accuracy of the scale, but the man's honesty was sustained by a verse from the Koran: "Lo! He over all things is watching." Smith suggests that this verse in the Koran "became true" in the person's life. In a similar way Smith says of Christianity that it "is not true absolutely, impersonally, statically: rather, it can *become* true, if and as you and I appropriate it to ourselves and interiorize it."[10]

If Smith is right, then we do not have to ask "Which religion is true?" They can all be true, in the sense that they all can give rise to "true lives." To look at religions as offering competing theories is a mistake.

Smith's view contains a deep insight, but the insight is accompanied by some confusion. He is quite right to stress that religious truth must be personally appropriated. I agree that in one sense of the word "true" one might appropriately speak of a person's life being true. Furthermore, no strict, necessary correlation binds the objective truth of a proposition and the "truth" of the life of an adherent to that proposition. It is conceivable that a person might believe objectively correct religious truths, yet personally live "falsely" because of a lack of interiorization of that truth. Furthermore, a person who believes objectively false propositions may still have some truth in his life, for it is possible for a person to be better than his theories.

None of this implies, however, that religions do not make competing truth-claims. It is possible for one religion to be objectively true in the sense that the major portion of its propositional claims are correct, while those of its competitors are false. Nor is this objective truth unimportant. If it is false that "Allah is watching over all things," then in an important sense the Himalayan fruit seller is deceived. Should he come to discover the objective falsehood of this proposition, this may affect the "truth" of his life.

Similarly, it makes no sense to say of Christianity that it has no objective truth status. If a person believes Jesus is the Son of God, it *is* all-important for her to interiorize this, as Smith says. But if Jesus is *not* really the Son of God, then it is a mistake for her to interiorize this. And it is hard to see how this *proposition* could become true for an individual merely by her accepting and appropriating this truth. The believer in Jesus does not believe that she has the power to make Jesus the Son of God or deny Jesus that status by her manner of believing. Rather, she believes that it is because Jesus really is the Son of God that she should believe in him and act on that belief.

The second strategy for eliminating the conflict between religions comes from John Hick. He differs from Smith in admitting that religions do make objective truth-claims and that these claims at least apparently conflict. Hick suggests, however, that the differences may be merely apparent. His basic idea is that God "in himself" is an infinite reality, "and as such transcends the grasp of the human mind."[11] Perhaps the apparently conflicting views the various religions have developed about God are like the apparently conflicting descriptions of an elephant produced by a group of blind people. The various religions all present "images of the divine, each expressing some aspect or range of aspects and yet none by itself fully and exhaustively corresponding to the infinite nature of the ultimate reality."[12] The apparent differences are due to the differing interpretations humans have placed on their experience of the divine, which are due to the different cultural and historical circumstances which have conditioned the experiences.[13] Hick calls for a new dialog between the world religions on this basis, a dialog which will hopefully resolve their apparent disagreements.

Hick's approach has much appeal. It does seem likely that the religious experiences of diverse cultures would contain true insights about God, and I heartily support Hick's call for dialog among the world's religions. A person committed to a particular faith need not regard all other faiths as completely wrong. Indeed, there may be many points of similarity, as is obviously the case with the great theistic religions, for example.

I question, however, whether the disagreements between the world's religions can be resolved as easily as Hick suggests. First, Hick's proposal implies that we must become skeptics about God in the final analysis. We do not really know God as he is, for God as he is "transcends human thought." In what sense then are our human images true images of *God*? Is any image truer than any other? If it is equally correct to think of God as a person who is capable of answering prayers and performing miracles and as an impersonal reality with no will or self-consciousness, then what view of God would be incorrect? The term "God" here threatens to become so nebulous as to lose all sense.

Second, Hick's proposal is not quite what it seems. On the

surface he seems to say that all religions could be true. But what about the "exclusive" claims made by various religions? Christianity, for example, says that Jesus is uniquely the Son of God and that salvation comes only through him. How can such a claim be reconciled with Hindu and Buddhist views, which might admit Jesus is *a* revealer of God and *a* path to salvation but could never admit the Christian claims?

Hick's response to this problem is revealing. He simply says that Christians must abandon their traditional belief in the doctrine of the Incarnation. It appears, then, that it is not the case that the religions of the world are all compatible as they stand. Rather, Hick is proposing to Christians that they modify their faith to make it compatible with other faiths.

If a person is a Christian, whether he should be willing to modify his faith in this way depends on the evidence he possesses for his faith. What is his basis for believing that Jesus is uniquely God? Traditionally, Christians have held this conviction on the basis of their acceptance of the Bible as a special, authoritative revelation from God.

Hick's proposal draws us back to the basic issue of how one knows religious truth. If special authoritative revelation is impossible, or if in fact one has never occurred, then something like Hick's view would be plausible. His position is the natural development of what was termed (in chapter five) the liberal view of revelation.[14] If, however, one holds that mankind's natural knowledge of God is inadequate, distorted by sin, and that a special revelation from God is required if we are to truly know God, then Hick's proposal seems dubious. Hick is in effect assuming, in Pelagian fashion, the essential ability of mankind to know God and be on good terms with him. If one believes that this assumption is dubious, then Hick's proposal will also appear dubious.

It is important, however, to recognize that someone who chooses to believe in the Bible as specially authoritative has not necessarily rejected reason. The questions whether a revelation could be authoritative and, if so, whether one has occurred can be rationally discussed. It is conceivable that reason might recognize that its ability to come to know God, operating within its natural abilities, is severely limited, and might see the need and value of a special revelation. Furthermore, reason can and must evaluate rival candidates to be such a revelation.

If someone is committed to an exclusivist religion, does this mean he is intolerant or arrogant? I do not think so. True tolerance and respect require a recognition of genuine differences. Genuine dialog likewise begins with a cordial admission of differences and a willingness to respect sincere disagreement.

Are there situations in which a religious believer (or unbeliever) ought to change his beliefs and "convert" to some other perspective? If the process of rationally testing one's faith described earlier in this chapter is to be more than a charade, clearly this must be a real possibility.

A religious believer who is convinced that her faith is true is not necessarily arrogant. She can, without giving up her convictions, admit her fallibility and appreciate the perspectives of others. If she is a Christian and holds to her faith on the basis of special revelation, she cannot be arrogant. For she recognizes that the knowledge she has of God is not the result of her own cleverness but is, in fact, made possible through her recognition of her own weakness. And if she feels compelled to share her faith with others, it may not be a sign of arrogant pride or imperialism but rather the result of a humble desire for others to know the truth.

Notes

Chapter 1: What Is Philosophy of Religion?

[1]*Fideism* as I have defined it is primarily a view which I have encountered among students and ordinary religious believers. It is not meant to be a precise statement of the views of any particular theologian or philosopher. An astute reader will no doubt notice, however, that as a general tendency fideism has some similarity to what is sometimes termed *presuppositionalism.* Thus, views which resemble the fideist view at certain points may be found in the writings of Cornelius Van Til and Gordon Clark and, in a different theological vein, Karl Barth. The views of these men are, however, more complicated, subtle and qualified than those of any simple fideist.

[2]A good introduction to the theory of knowledge is the first book in this series, David Wolfe's *Epistemology: The Justification of Belief* (Downers Grove, Ill.: InterVarsity Press, 1982).

[3]In addition to "strong" foundationalism there is also a "weak" foundationalism, which claims that some of our knowledge is properly basic or foundational to the rest, but does not claim that this foundational knowledge is known with absolute certainty. Rather our basic knowledge is seen as fallible, subject to correction and revision. Weak foundationalism is consistent with the approach taken in this book.

[4]Thomas S. Kuhn, *The Structure of Scientific Revolutions,* 2d ed. (Chicago: Univ. of Chicago Press, 1970).

[5]See David Hume's *An Enquiry Concerning Human Understanding* (Indianapolis: Hackett Pub., 1977), sect. 12, p. 103.

Chapter 2: The Theistic God: The Project of Natural Theology

[1]For a good introduction to the current debate on these issues see Ronald H. Nash, *The Concept of God* (Grand Rapids, Mich.: Zondervan, 1983). For a fine, technical treatment see Richard Swinburne, *The Coherence of Theism* (Oxford: Oxford Univ. Press, 1977).

[2]George Mavrodes, *Belief in God* (New York: Random House, 1970), pp. 17-48.

[3]Ibid., pp. 33-34. I have updated Mavrodes' example by substituting Reagan for Nixon.

[4]Ibid., p. 40.

Chapter 3: Classical Arguments for God's Existence

[1]Anselm's *Proslogion* is available in a number of editions. The crucial sections on the ontological argument are found in chapters two and three and are included in many anthologies in the philosophy of religion, including the excellent one edited by William I. Rowe and William J. Wainwright, *Philosophy of Religion: Selected Readings* (New York: Harcourt Brace Jovanovich, 1973), pp. 103-5.

[2]See Norman Malcolm, "Anselm's Ontological Arguments," *Philosophical Review* (January 1960). This article can be found in John Hick, ed., *The Existence of God* (New York: Macmillan, 1964), pp. 47-70.

[3]See Alvin Plantinga, *God, Freedom, and Evil* (Grand Rapids, Mich.: Eerdmans, 1977), p. 112.

[4]See Karl Barth, *Anselm: Fides Quaerens Intellectum,* trans. Ian Robertson (Richmond, Va.: John Knox Press, 1960). Key selections from this work can be found in *The Many-Faced Argument,* ed. John Hick and Arthur C. McGill (New York: Macmillan, 1967), pp. 119-61.

[5]Actually, some philosophers make a distinction between first-cause arguments and cosmological arguments. This distinction is not particularly helpful in my opinion. Usually the distinction is really between two different kinds of cosmological arguments employing different concepts of causality.

[6]See Stuart Hackett, *The Resurrection of Theism* (Grand Rapids, Mich.: Baker, 1982) for an example of the denial of an actual infinite temporal series. The historical roots of this view have been traced by William Craig in *The Kalam Cosmological Argument* (London: Macmillan, 1979). Craig also defends the argument against various objections.

[7]See William Hasker, *Metaphysics* (Downers Grove, Ill.: InterVarsity Press, 1983), pp. 116-17, for an example of the claim that the big bang theory supports theism. (Also see Hasker's footnote for additional reading on the subject.)

[8]See Paul Edwards, "The Cosmological Argument," reprinted in Rowe and Wainwright, *Philosophy of Religion,* pp. 136-48.

[9]See Albert Camus, "An Absurd Reasoning," in *The Myth of Sisyphus and Other Essays* (New York: Random House, 1955), pp. 3-48.

[10]St. Thomas Aquinas's "Five Ways" are found in his *Summa Theologica* 1. 2. 3. This section is included in numerous anthologies. My quotation is taken from Rowe and Wainwright, eds., *Philosophy of Religion: Selected Readings,* p. 119. An inexpensive edition of the *Summa* is available from Image Books, general editor, Thomas Gilby, O.P.

[11]David Hume, *Dialogues Concerning Natural Religion,* ed. Norman Kemp Smith (Indianapolis: Bobbs-Merrill, 1947), pp. 170-81.

[12]Ibid., pp. 148-50.

[13]Ibid., pp. 146, 174.

[14]Ibid., pp. 182-85.

[15]Ibid., pp. 165-69. Hume also objects that the designer would not be wholly good because of imperfections in the design. We will consider this problem in chapter six, which deals with the problem of evil.

[16]See Richard Swinburne, *The Existence of God* (Oxford: Oxford Univ. Press, 1979), pp. 141-42.

[17]For a detailed discussion of Kant's argument and its structure, see my *Subjectivity and Religious Belief* (1978; reprint ed., Washington, D.C.: Univ. Press of America, 1982), pp. 15-73.

[18]C. S. Lewis, *Mere Christianity* (London: Collins, 1955), pp. 15-38.

[19]See Robert Adams, "A Modified Divine Command Theory of Ethical Wrongness," in *Divine Commands and Morality,* ed. Paul Helm (Oxford Oxford Univ. Press, 1981), pp. 83-108.

[20]Thomas Aquinas, *On the Truth of the Catholic Faith (Summa Contra Gentiles)* (Garden City, N.Y.: Doubleday and Company, 1955), pp. 67-68 (1.4).

Chapter 4: Religious Experience

[1]Ramanuja's thought would be an excellent example. For discussion of Ramanuja which bears on this issue see Peter A. Bertocci, "The Logic of Creationism, Advaita, and Visishtadvaita: A Critique," in *The Person God Is* (New York: Humanities Press, 1970), pp. 223-37, and Stuart C. Hackett, *Oriental Philosophy: A Westerner's Guide to Eastern Thought* (Madison, Wis.: Univ. of Wisconsin Press, 1979), pp. 157-78.

[2]Alasdair MacIntyre claims this in his essay "Visions," in *New Essays in Philosophical Theology,* ed. Antony Flew and Alasdair MacIntyre (New York: Macmillan, 1964), p. 256.

[3]Much of what follows draws heavily on George Mavrodes, *Belief in God,* pp.

49-89.

Chapter 5: Special Acts of God: Revelations and Miracles

[1]Immanuel Kant, "What Is Enlightenment?" in *Critique of Practical Reason and Other Writings in Moral Philosophy,* trans. and ed. Lewis White Beck (Chicago: Univ. of Chicago Press, 1949), pp. 286-92.

[2]David Hume, "Of Miracles," in *An Enquiry Concerning Human Understanding,* p. 77n, italics his.

[3]For example, John Hick forthrightly declares, "If miracle is defined as a breach of natural law, one can declare a priori that there are no miracles." See his *Philosophy of Religion,* 2d ed. (Englewood Cliffs, N.J.: Prentice-Hall, 1973), p. 46.

[4]Theists do not have to interpret natural laws as merely descriptive of actual events, however. That is, they can acknowledge that laws of nature describe not merely what does in fact happen, but also what *would* happen if other conditions had occurred. However, such laws can still be interpreted theistically as *descriptive* of God's normal "patterning" of the universe.

[5]Hume, "Of Miracles," p. 76.

[6]Ibid., p. 77.

[7]See Hume's chapter "Of Probability," in *An Enquiry Concerning Human Understanding,* pp. 37-39.

[8]Hume, "Of Miracles," p. 79.

[9]Ibid., pp. 78-79.

[10]Ibid., p. 81.

[11]This seems to be the line of thought advanced by John Hick in the passage quoted in note 3.

[12]Patrick Nowell-Smith, "Miracles," in Flew and MacIntyre, eds., *New Essays in Philosophical Theology,* pp. 243-53.

[13]See Richard Swinburne, *The Concept of Miracle* (London: Macmillan, 1970), esp. pp. 23-32.

[14]See David Wolfe's *Epistemology* for a good discussion of the epistemological procedure whereby someone could reasonably decide such a question.

Chapter 6: Objections to Theism: Modernity, Science and Evil

[1]Rudolf Bultmann et al., *Kerygma and Myth* (New York: Harper & Row, 1967), p. 5.

[2]H. H. Farmer, *Towards Belief in God* (New York: Macmillan, 1943), pp. 145-67.

[3]J. L. Mackie, "Evil and Omnipotence," in Rowe and Wainwright, eds., *Philosophy of Religion: Selected Readings,* p. 206; reprinted from *Mind* 64, no.

254 (April 1955).

[4]Ibid., p. 207.

[5]See chapter two of William Hasker's *Metaphysics* for a good discussion of this issue and defense of free will.

[6]See Genesis 3:17-19 and Romans 8:19-23.

[7]For two recent, somewhat novel responses to the problem, see Richard Swinburne, *The Existence of God*, pp. 200-224; and Bruce Reichenbach, *Evil and a Good God* (New York: Fordham Univ. Press, 1982), esp. pp. 87-120, which presents an interesting theodicy for natural evil.

[8]For more on this, see the discussion of Basil Mitchell's parable of the "Mysterious Stranger," in the next chapter, pp. 149-50.

Chapter 7: The Problem of Religious Language

[1]A. J. Ayer, *Language, Truth and Logic* (New York: Dover Pub., 1946), pp. 115-16.

[2]For discussions of the many attempts (and failures) to develop a plausible version of the verifiability theory, see Carl G. Hempel, "The Empiricist Criterion of Meaning," reprinted in *Logical Positivism*, ed. A. J. Ayer (1959; reprint ed., Westport, Conn.: Greenwood Press, 1978), pp. 108-29, also printed under the title "Problems and Changes in the Empiricist Criterion of Meaning," in *Semantics and the Philosophy of Language*, ed. Leonard Linsky (Urbana: Univ. of Illinois Press, 1952), pp. 163-85; see also Alvin Plantinga, *God and Other Minds* (Ithaca, N.Y.: Cornell Univ. Press, 1967), pp. 156-68.

[3]See Kai Nielsen, *An Introduction to the Philosophy of Religion* (New York: St. Martin's Press, 1982), esp. pp. 18-19 and chap. six.

[4]Antony Flew and others, "Theology and Falsification," in Flew and MacIntyre, *New Essays in Philosophical Theology*, p. 96.

[5]R. M. Hare in ibid., pp. 99-100.

[6]R. B. Braithwaite, "An Empiricist's View of the Nature of Religious Beliefs," reprinted in Hick, *Existence of God*, pp. 229-52.

[7]For a brief introduction to Tillich's theory, see his "Religious Symbols and Our Knowledge of God," reprinted in Rowe and Wainwright, *Philosophy of Religion*, pp. 479-88.

[8]Basil Mitchell, "Theology and Falsification," in Flew and MacIntyre, *New Essays in Philosophical Theology*, pp. 103-5.

[9]John Hick, "Theology and Verification," *Theology Today* 17, no. 1 (April 1960), reprinted in Rowe and Wainwright, *Philosophy of Religion*, pp. 437-52.

[10]Ibid., pp. 448-49.

[11]Ludwig Wittgenstein, *Philosophical Investigations*, trans. G. E. M. Anscombe (New York: Macmillan, 1948), p. 11e, italics his.

¹²Ibid., italics his.

¹³Kai Nielsen, "Wittgensteinian Fideism," in *Philosophy* 42, no. 161 (1967):191-209.

¹⁴D. Z. Phillips, *Death and Immortality* (London: Macmillan, 1970).

¹⁵Aquinas's theory is developed in part 1, question 13, of his *Summa Theologica*.

¹⁶For a brief example of such an argument, see William Blackstone, *The Problem of Religious Knowledge* (New York: Prentice-Hall, 1963), pp. 121-22. For a more extended defense of the idea that analogical predication depends on univocal predication, see Paul Hayner, "Analogical Predication," *The Journal of Philosophy* 55 (25 September 1958):855-62.

¹⁷For interesting treatments of scientific models, pointing out implications for theological discourse, see Ian T. Ramsey, *Models and Mystery* (London: Oxford Univ. Press, 1974), and Ian Barbour, *Myths, Models, and Paradigms* (New York: Harper & Row, 1974).

¹⁸I. M. Crombie, "Theology and Falsification," in Flew and MacIntyre, *New Essays in Philosophical Theology,* pp. 109-30.

Chapter 8: Religious Pluralism and Personal Faith

¹Once more I would recommend David Wolfe's *Epistemology* for a good introductory treatment.

²For an excellent sketch of the problems which beset foundationalism, see Nicholas Wolterstorff, *Reason Within the Bounds of Religion* (Grand Rapids, Mich.: Eerdmans, 1976), esp. pp. 24-51.

³See Kuhn, *Structure of Scientific Revolutions;* and Stephen Toulmin, *Foresight and Understanding* (New York: Harper & Row, 1963).

⁴Basil Mitchell, *The Justification of Religious Belief* (New York: Oxford Univ. Press, 1981). See particularly pp. 45-57 for a fuller account of what follows.

⁵Ibid., pp. 39-45.

⁶H. H. Price, *Belief* (New York: Humanities Press, 1969). Price calls these two theories the "occurrence analysis" and the "dispositional analysis."

⁷Luke 18:18-23.

⁸Wilfred Cantwell Smith, "A Human View of Truth," in *Truth and Dialogue in World Religions: Conflicting Truth-Claims,* ed. John Hick (Philadelphia: Westminster Press, 1974), pp. 20-44.

⁹Wilfred Cantwell Smith, *Questions of Religious Truth,* pp. 89-90; quoted in John Hick, "The Outcome: Dialogue into Truth," in *Truth and Dialogue in World Religions,* p. 146.

¹⁰Smith, *Questions of Religious Truth,* p. 68, quoted in Hick, *Truth and Dialogue in World Religions,* p. 145.

¹¹John Hick, *God and the Universe of Faiths* (New York: St. Martin's Press,

1973), p. 139.

[12]Ibid., p. 140.

[13]Ibid., p. 146.

[14]The claim here is that Hick's view logically presupposes something like the liberal view of revelation, not that Hick would himself espouse this view. In his book *Philosophy of Religion,* Hick defends a version of the nonpropositional view of revelation. I do not know whether he has since modified that view. My point is simply that Hick's view of world religions seems to rule out the possibility of one religion's possessing a revelation which would have special authority over others. The route to knowing God would then seem to be through the general religious experience of mankind, and the distinction between general and special revelation is eroded. This I take to be the heart of the liberal view of revelation.

Further Reading

The notes offer a wealth of suggestions for further reading, but the following represent those I consider especially valuable. Most of these books contain extensive bibliographies.

General Introductions

Purtill, Richard L. *Thinking about Religion: A Philosophical Introduction to Religion.* Englewood Cliffs, N.J.: Prentice-Hall, 1978.

Rowe, William L. *Philosophy of Religion: An Introduction.* Belmont, Calif.: Wadsworth Pub. Co., 1978.

Anthologies

Brody, Baruch A. *Readings in the Philosophy of Religion: An Analytic Approach.* Englewood Cliffs, N.J.: Prentice-Hall, 1974.

Rowe, William L., and Wainwright, William J. *Philosophy of Religion: Selected Readings.* New York: Harcourt Brace Jovanovich, 1973.

On the Concept of God

Nash, Ronald H. *The Concept of God.* Grand Rapids, Mich.: Zondervan, 1983.

Swinburne, Richard. *The Coherence of Theism.* Oxford: Oxford Univ. Press, 1977.

On the Theistic Arguments and Religious Experience

Mavrodes, George. *Belief in God.* 1970. Reprint. Lanham, Md.: Univ. Press of America, 1981.

Swinburne, Richard. *The Existence of God.* Oxford: Oxford Univ. Press, 1979.

Miracles and Special Revelation

Brown, Colin. *Miracles and the Critical Mind.* Grand Rapids, Mich.: Eerdmans, 1984.

Lewis, C. S. *Miracles: A Preliminary Study.* New York: Macmillan Pub. Co., 1947.

Swinburne, Richard. *The Concept of Miracle.* London: Macmillan, 1970.

The Problem of Evil

Mavrodes, George. *Belief in God.* 1970. Reprint. Lanham, Md.: Univ. Press of America, 1981.

Peterson, Michael. *Evil and the Christian God.* Grand Rapids, Mich.: Baker Book House, 1982.

Plantinga, Alvin. *God, Freedom, and Evil.* Grand Rapids, Mich.: Eerdmans, 1977.

Faith, Reason and Commitment

Mitchell, Basil. *The Justification of Religious Belief.* Oxford: Oxford Univ. Press, 1981.

Plantinga, Alvin, and Wolterstorff, Nicholas, eds. *Faith and Rationality: Reason and Belief in God.* Notre Dame, Ind.: Univ. of Notre Dame Press, 1983.